Recipes for Redemption

Recipes *for* Redemption

A Companion Cookbook to

A Cup *of* Redemption

Carole Bumpus

She Writes Press

Published 2015
Printed in the United States of America
ISBN: 978-1-63152-824-8
Library of Congress Control Number: 2015935547

Book design by Stacey Aaronson

For information, address:
She Writes Press
1563 Solano Ave #546
Berkeley, CA 94707

She Writes Press is a division of SparkPoint Studio, LLC.

Cuisine Pauvre

"So, you are interested in learning how to prepare our cuisine, *n'est ce pas*?" Marcelle peered over the top of her wine glass as she spoke.

"*Oui,* Madame, I would love to learn what makes your cuisine world-famous; your *haute-cuisine,*" Kate said.

"Our *haute-cuisine*?" Marcelle bit into her cheese and bread. A twinkle flitted through her dark eyes.

"*Oui,* but more than '*haute-cuisine*' I would prefer learning the fine art of traditional French cooking."

"Well, Madame, our traditional cooking is rarely considered fine, but we certainly keep a respectable '*cuisine pauvre.*'"

Kate was brought up short with this French term. She turned quizzically toward Sophie.

"Kate, '*cuisine pauvre*' means 'poor kitchen' and refers to a traditional-type of peasant cooking. These are the recipes that have been handed down through the many, many generations in our family and this is the type of cooking *Maman* taught me."

—*A Cup of Redemption, a Novel*

North Sea
UNITED KINGDOM
NETHERLANDS
GERMANY
BELGIUM
LUXEMBOURG
English Channel
Nord-Pas-de-Calais
Albert
Haute-Normandie
Rouen
Picardie
Ste. Barbe
Verdun
Metz
Alsace
Seine
PARIS
Basse-Normandie
Mont Saint-Michel
Île-de-France
Champagne-Ardennes
Lorraine
Brittany
River
Pays de la Loire
Vannes
Orléans
Angers
Loire
River
Centre
Burgundy
Franche-Comté
SWITZ.
Poitou Charles
Evaux-les-Bain
Vichy
Fontanières
Lyon
ATLANTIC OCEAN
Limousin
Clermont-Ferrand
Rhône-Alpes
Auvergne
River
ITALY
Bordeaux
Rhône
Garonne
Aquitaine
River
Provence-Alpes-Côte-d'Azur
Midi-Pyrénées
MONACO
Languedoc Roussillon
ANDORRA
Mediterranean Sea
SPAIN
N
0
100 mi
0
100 km

On Peasant Foods

Antoine Gilly, one of the world's foremost French chefs and restaurateurs, once said:

> I am not sure that the food served by the simple farm people of France does not rank as high as any, including the haute cuisine that we rattle on about. If taste, imagination, originality and simplicity are the prime ingredients of fine cookery, go thou gourmet to the peasant as I have and discover all of these qualities. Then make your own decision, whether you would prefer lunch or dinner at the elegant Lasserre in Paris or at home with farmer Pierre near Dijon at his oak table scrubbed oyster white or at his country inn, eating the favorite dish of the region and drinking the local wine from a carafe.
>
> —*Antoine Gilly's Feast of France: A Cookbook of Masterpieces in French Cuisine* (1971), page 341

Welcome to *Recipes for Redemption: A Companion Cookbook to A Cup of Redemption.* Pour yourself a cup of coffee, seat yourself at your kitchen table and take out your copy of *A Cup of Redemption* (or pick one up with this cookbook). Surely, you will want to follow along as each chapter of your companion cookbook corresponds to and draws from the tantalizing excerpts found in the same chapters of the historical novel.

Within, you will find the long-awaited and much-promised recipes—all traditional French—culled from the very pages, the times, and the regional influences you found in my historical novel *A Cup of Redemption.* Told through the voices of the three main characters—Marcelle, Sophie, and Kate—you will find the recipes are taught in the way these women learned them: at the knees of their mothers and grandmothers. Whether '*cuisine pauvre*' (peasant cooking), 'war food' from WWII, or simple family favorites, each recipe is carefully described and footnoted with interesting, often amusing culinary notes. Flavored with witty repartee and slathered with common sense, you will find the following pages filled with the same heart, soul, humor, and delectable delight you found in *A Cup of Redemption.* And for an additional *amuse-bouche,* I invite you to enjoy some excerpts of my up-coming series, *Savoring the Olde Ways.*

Bon appétit!

Carole Bumpus

Contents

Centre
Burgundy
Montluçon
Vichy
Fontanières
Limousin
Puy De
Dôme
Clermont-Ferrand
Lyon
Auvergne
River
Rhône
Rhône-
Alpes
Midi- Pyrénées
Languedoc
Roussillon
N
0
25 mi
0
25 km

Chapter One

A Flood of Memories:
Omelette aux Champignons et au Fromage
and
Crêpes ou Galettes

Omelette aux Champignons et au Fromage
(Sophie's Mushroom and Cheese Omelet)
from the Auvergne Region

Sophie fussed about the kitchen, searching through one cupboard after another, peering into the fridge, all in hopes of finding a scrap of something to eat. *I should have eaten more at the wake . . .* She had no idea what she would find, as her mother's death in France had come only hours after her own arrival from the States. And there had been so much to take care of for the funeral that she barely remembered how long she had been there. Tucked back in the corner of the refrigerator was a blue crock of eggs. A small container of boletus mushrooms was hidden on a shelf in the door along with a scrap of Brie and some butter. *Une omelette aux champignons et au fromage,* she surmised.

With omelet essentials in hand, she closed the refrigerator door with her foot, just as the cheese, mushrooms, and butter tumbled out of her hands and onto the counter. Hanging on to the eggs, she pulled out the omelet pan—the very one her mother had taught her to use—and set it on the stove to heat. Oh, the laughter they used to share—as her mother patiently taught her and her brother, Julien, how to break an egg or how to make an omelet. And then to make crêpes . . . *Crêpes.* She laughed. Oh, the fun all the families would have together during *Chandeleur,* the Festival of Lights. She couldn't recall the reason for the religious holiday, but the laughter would ring through the air each time they were given turns flipping crêpes high into the air. The goal was to catch it back on the paddle without dropping the crêpe or sticking it to the ceiling. *Wait!* She stopped for a moment to think. *That's it! We were to hold a gold coin in one hand while tossing the crêpe with the other, all in order to win good fortune or money. Not an easy task when you are laughing,* she chortled out loud. While melting a knob of butter to sauté the mushrooms, she quickly broke two eggs into a bowl, added a dash of water, and lightly whisked them together. She cocked her head and listened. The very moment the mushrooms had finished sizzling, she poured the eggs into the pan.

Quickly tilting the pan back and forth, she let her thoughts again drift back to the first conversations her mother had had with Kate. *Could* Maman *have wanted to share her secrets with me through our conversations with Kate?* Kate knew enough French, but of course, Sophie still had to translate many of her mother's words. It was during those translations that she became painfully aware of the depth of information her mother was revealing. And Kate hadn't wanted to miss a word or syllable. She had been captivated by her mother's story, asking more and more questions.

Anguish shot through her and surprised her with its force. Sophie shook her head in disbelief and choked down another swallow of bad wine. She minced the chunk of Brie, dumped it into the egg mixture, and deftly lifted one edge of the omelet, folding it over. Within moments she slid the omelet onto a plate and called it good. Sophie picked up a fork and her glass of wine and sat down at the kitchen table. She inhaled the eggs almost before they cooled.

—*A Cup of Redemption,* pages 12–13

One of my favorite old cookbooks is *Antoine Gilly's Feast of France.* Monsieur Gilly dedicates his cookbook to his dear French grandmother, who raised him in the region of Burgundy. And in the section "Eggs," he begins a lengthy description of how to master an omelet: "I recommend that when learning to make an *omelette,* you invest in four dozen eggs and practice. Nothing else will make you an expert—not words from the skilled, not observations (although it does help to watch an expert at work), only breaking eggs and going at it makes the difference."

2 eggs

2 tablespoons heavy cream or water

1/4 cup (1/2 stick) sweet butter (do not use salted butter or margarine; they cause too-rapid browning)

Salt and pepper to taste

"Break the eggs in a mixing bowl and add the cream [Sophie had only water available] and about half the butter, cut in small pieces. Sprinkle with salt and pepper. Beat the eggs with a kitchen fork, lifting up with each stroke to aerate, no more than 12 strokes for each egg. Do not overdo this beating. If you do, the eggs will be thin and tough in cooking.

"Place the *omelette* pan (one only used for eggs) on high heat. Put a piece of butter on a fork and hold it against the inside of the pan. If it instantly sizzles, add a generous piece of butter to the pan waiting until it foams and turns white. Tilt the pan around so the butter covers its entire surface, sides included. Do all this quickly. The eggs should go in when the butter reaches its peak heat—before burning. The butter should not be brown or it will color the *omelette.*

"If the butter is at the right heat, the eggs will sizzle sharply as you pour them in. Almost instantly, they will begin to solidify, forming a foamy edge around the pan. Immediately stir eggs in a circular motion with the flat bottom of the fork, spreading the eggs about the pan. Holding the handle with the left hand (unless left-handed), agitate the pan, moving the quickly-forming *omelette* back and forth. Stirring speeds the coagulation, and the agitation of the pan prevents sticking. Now stop stirring. Shake pan with both hands, raising it slightly above heat. At this point, I hit the handle of the pan sharply with the heel of my hand, which causes the far edge of the *omelette* to fold. If this doesn't work for you, lift the pan so that the liquid egg runs to end of pan where it will solidify. At the same time, slip your fork under the side of *omelette* near you and lift the edge, 'helping' it to make the correct fold. When the liquid is nearly solid, flip the near edge over with the fork, and continue to shake the pan so the eggs won't stick. Then prepare to tilt the *omelette* out of the pan.

"Holding a warm serving plate in your left hand and, grasping the handle of the pan so that it is to your right, rest edge of pan on the plate, off center enough so the *omelette* will land in the middle of the plate. Now, simultaneously tilt pan and plate about 45 degrees against one another. In a fast motion, flip the pan upside down over the plate and the folded *omelette* will drop properly in place.

"Keep the serving plates warm. *Omelettes* cool and harden quickly. I also rub soft butter over the *omelette* just before I serve it. Important! Serve immediately! If you dawdle over serving, your skillful egg-envelopes will taste not unlike those in which you mail a letter."

—Adapted from *Antoine Gilly's Feast of France: A Cookbook of Masterpieces in French Cuisine,* pg 104

Variation:

Omelet with Sautéed Mushrooms and Brie

Begin by slicing two or three brown mushrooms (boleti) very thinly and sautéing them first in the pan with the butter. (See above.) To add the Brie as Sophie did, I suggest you chop it very finely or grate 1/4 cup of it into the egg mixture before pouring this into the pan. *Très bon!*

Crêpes ou Galettes Bretonnes
from the Brittany region

If Marcelle was to teach you to make crêpes or galettes from Brittany, she might tell you that when her *grand'mère* prepared them over the fire, she'd say, "Marcelle, now remember, it is customary for a bride to throw the first galette baked in her new house onto the cupboard as a tribute to the previous residents of the house. This tradition secures domestic happiness and protection for her offspring."

"Did *Maman* do that?" Marcelle would push her grandmother for information, always hoping that a new morsel would slip out. Instead, a crisp, lacy, yet tender crêpe was flipped off the pan and onto her waiting plate. "Get butter on that, *ma chérie,* before it turns cold."

MAKES TEN 6-INCH CRÊPES

1 cup all-purpose flour
1/2 cup milk
1/2 cup water
1/4 teaspoon salt
2 large eggs
2 tablespoons clarified butter, melted, plus more for the pan

In a medium bowl, sift together the flour and salt. Make a well in the center. Whisk together the milk, water, and eggs in another medium bowl. Pour the milk mixture into the center of the well, slowly whisking in the flour from the sides. Add 2 tablespoons clarified butter and whisk to combine.

Strain the mixture through a fine-mesh sieve into a mixing bowl. Cover with plastic wrap and chill in the refrigerator for 30 minutes.

Remove the batter from the refrigerator. Heat a 6-inch crêpe pan or nonstick frying pan over medium-high heat. Brush with clarified butter, and heat until very hot. Add a couple of tablespoons of batter, turning and swirling the batter in the pan to completely coat the bottom. Cook until brown on the bottom, 1 to 2 minutes. Flip the crêpe with a spatula and cook golden-brown on the other side, about 1 minute more. Repeat with the remaining batter. As you continue, you will need to use less butter in the crêpe pan.

These crêpes can be used with either sweet or savory fillings. Savory galettes can be filled with anything from a fried egg to ham and cheese to sautéed vegetables. Sweet galettes/crêpes are lightly sweetened with warmed jam or sprinkled with confectioners' sugar and served as dessert or as an after-school snack.

Galettes au Sarrasin
(Buckwheat Crêpes)
from the Brittany region

Buckwheat, not a grain in the true sense, is related to knotgrass. Its original home is Asia, from whence it spread toward both Russia and the Middle East. It came to France with the Crusaders, and because it was such a dark color it was called Sarasin or Saracen. The buckwheat galette, once called *jalet* in Brittany, is considered humankind's oldest food, and was originally baked as a substitute for bread on a hot flat stone.

> The buckwheat "galette," or crêpe, is the true crêpe of Brittany, the one that is still a staple... In the old days, every farmwife had her billig, a three-legged crêpe pan that stood right over the fire. She would spend all day Friday—a meatless day in the Catholic Church—making galettes on the billig and mounding them on the table as she deftly scooped them off. After every third crêpe or so, she would take a rag that sat in a pot of lard and egg yolks and run it over the billig, to oil it for the following galettes. Many crêperies in Brittany use the same antiquated, though efficient, system.
>
> —Susan Herrmann Loomis,
> *The French Farmhouse Cookbook,* page 293

MAKES ABOUT 10 CRÊPES

1 3/4 cups plus 1 tablespoon buckwheat flour

1/2 teaspoon sea salt

2 1/4 cups water

2 large eggs

1 tablespoon melted butter

Prepare the same way as previous crêpe recipes.

CHAPTER TWO

Pâté de Pommes de Terre

AND

Oeufs à la Neige

Pâté de Pommes de Terre Grand'mère
(Marcelle's Grandmother's Potato-Filled Pie)
from the Auvergne Region

"What foods did I prepare? In France?" Marcelle echoed the question. She threw her head back and laughed, her deeply resonant voice filling the room. But then she sat back in her chair as her eyes lighted on the birds fluttering outside the sliding glass door. Kate was surprised at her laughter, but followed her gaze to see what had caught her attention. The California hills, just beyond her backyard, were vibrant green from recent winter rains, and the birds were having a heyday. She imagined Marcelle's mind fluttering too, back through the cobwebs of her past. Through the glass tabletop Marcelle's shoeless feet swung under the chair, back and forth, to and fro. Marcelle stretched her back, picked up her fork, and sampled the lemon tart.

"Mmm, *très bon,* madame." She swallowed. "Maybe I should get *your* recipe." She paused. "Well, to answer your question," she began, her rich voice rising, "I never had to diet." She tossed her head back and laughed again as she licked lemon curd off her lips. She pulled her large brown sweater about herself as Sophie tittered at the old family joke. Clearly Marcelle Zabél had stories to tell.

"It was during World War II, you see," Marcelle began again, "and we had to forage in the fields for every potato, every carrot, even for an onion or two. We had a chicken once in a while, or a bit of rabbit. You know, some of the foods I learned to cook back in '43, I still prepare today, like *Pâté de Pommes de Terre.* You wanted recipes, *oui*? I'll be sure to give you that one."

—*A Cup of Redemption,* page 31

First of all, in this case a *pâté* is a pastry, so this is a basic potato-meat pie. Marcelle used a lard pastry dough, or *pâté au saindoux* (her very favorite).

Pâté de Pommes de Terre Grand'mère

(Pastry)

2 1/2 cups all-purpose flour

1 teaspoon salt

1 cup solid saindoux (lard) or 1/2 cup lard + 1/2 cup unsalted butter

1/3 cup plus 1 tablespoon ice water

In a bowl, cut the fat into the dry ingredients with a pastry blender. The end product should have the lard in pea-sized pieces and the rest of the mixture dry and powdery. Drizzle the ice water over the flour mixture as you mix with a rubber spatula. When the dough forms a ball, you have added enough water. If not add 1 to 2 more tablespoons of water. Form a ball, wrap it in plastic wrap, and set in the refrigerator for at least 30 minutes.

Prepare as you would a regular piecrust (see chapter 21). This provides a top and bottom crust. Roll out the bottom crust and place it in a pie pan.

FILLING

1/4 cup chopped semi-salty *lardons* (thick bacon)

1 pound Yukon Gold potatoes, peeled and sliced into thin rounds

1/2 cup chopped onion

5 cloves garlic, finely chopped

Salt and pepper to taste

1 tablespoon chopped parsley

1 egg yolk beaten with 1 tablespoon water

Blanch the *lardons* (bacon) in boiling water for 3 minutes to diminish the saltiness. Then place them in a *sauteuse* (frying pan) to render the fat. Add the potatoes, onion, garlic, then salt and pepper to taste. When the filling is slightly golden, layer it into the bottom crust, sprinkle with the chopped parsley, place the top crust on, and crimp the edges. Glaze the *pâté* with the egg yolk mixture using a pastry brush. Bake in a preheated oven set at 350°F for 1 hour. Serve with a green salad. *Voilà!*

Oeufs à la Neige
(Eggs in Snow or *Ile Flottante* - Marcelle's Floating Island Dessert)
from France

Marcelle smiled and said, "Shall we prepare the Floating Island? It is quite easy. Nothing like your delicious lemon tart, Kate. Now, to begin with—" Marcelle pushed back from the table, scooting her feet back into her shoes. "—the French name for this dessert is *Oeufs à la Neige*. We will begin with two cups of milk and the peeling of one orange. Are you ready, Kate?"

Kate spun into action and produced the measured amount of milk and orange peeling. Sophie had prepared her well. Marcelle picked up a small copper pan and began to heat the milk with the rind, bringing it to a boil. In the meantime, she had Sophie beat the egg whites until they were stiff. Slowly Marcelle added confectioners' sugar and lemon juice into the mix, while Sophie continued beating the whites. Kate stood by taking notes.

—*A Cup of Redemption,* page 35

2 cups milk
4 eggs, separated
1 teaspoon lemon juice
Drop of vanilla extract
Peel of 1 orange
1/4 cup confectioners' sugar
1/2 cup granulated sugar
Pinch of salt

Bring the milk to a boil with the orange peel in a shallow pan. Reduce the heat under the milk to a simmer.

Meanwhile, beat the egg whites stiff. Slowly add the confectioners' sugar and the lemon juice, beating for 1 minute. With a tablespoon, scoop out the beaten whites, molding them into egg shapes.

Drop two or three spoonfuls of the whites into this pan (they expand as they cook). Cook 1 minute on each side, turning carefully. Remove with a slotted spoon and drain on cheesecloth or a white towel. Repeat until all the whites are used.

In a medium bowl, blend the egg yolks with the granulated sugar, vanilla, and salt, using a wooden spatula. Slowly pour the hot milk over, stirring rapidly with a wire whisk to prevent curdling. Return the mixture to the pan and simmer on a low fire for 3 minutes, stirring constantly. Watch carefully. The custard should be thick enough to coat the back of the spoon; do not overcook or it will curdle. Strain through a fine-mesh strainer into a deep serving dish of glass or porcelain and refrigerate.

When the custard is cold, arrange the egg whites on top. Decorate each egg white with a maraschino cherry or piece of candied fruit, or drizzle lightly spun caramelized sugar (below) over them all.

Sugar Caramel

1 cup water
1/2 cup sugar

Boil the sugar and water until the syrup becomes dark blond in color. (Do not let the sugar burn and the syrup darken too much, because it will become bitter.) Dip a fork into the syrup and carefully drizzle it over the Floating Island in strings a few minutes before serving.

As I began to re-create this recipe of Marcelle's I happened onto the exact measurements from, once again, one of my favorite cookbooks, *Antoine Gilly's Feast of France.* (Much easier to call on Antoine than to sort out the grams, kilograms, and other differences found in French cookbooks.) I also learned that the dessert names are sometimes interchangeable. *Ile Flottante* is the French name for 'Floating Island' and *Oeufs à la Niege* is the French name for 'Eggs in Snow'.

CHAPTER THREE

Casserole Auvergnate

(Jeannine's Stuffed Chicken with Sausage and Chestnuts)

from the Auvergne Region

Sophie spent the rest of the morning huddled in her bathrobe reading one page after another of her mother's journals, crying, then sorting through legal papers and reading through more letters. Thierry arrived later that afternoon looking as if he had just crawled out of bed. His dark curly hair was punked out on top and he looked ten years older than the previous day. Being under strict orders to deliver his wife's *Casserole Auvergnate* to Sophie, he had no choice. Sophie hadn't realized how hungry she was before he arrived, but she never could resist Jeannine's delicious sausage-and-chestnut-stuffed dish. What a treat! The succulent and savory aroma filled the small house and, thankfully, expunged the air of dead roses. Sophie's mouth watered as she set the platter on the kitchen counter and made a fresh pot of coffee.

"Oh, and a bottle of wine, too," Thierry said, slowly withdrawing it from deep within a pocket.

"How marvelous," she said as she turned to hug her brother. "Your wife certainly likes to spoil me, doesn't she? Is she joining us? Do you want to eat with me, drink with me, or do you just want some coffee?"

—*A Cup of Redemption,* pages 54–55

Stuffing

1 tablespoon vegetable oil
1 medium onion, peeled and chopped
1 cup crumbled sausage, about 1/2 pound
2 eggs, slightly beaten
1/2 cup chopped chestnuts
1 pound fresh spinach, trimmed, cooked, and drained
1 pound cured ham and/or lean salt pork, coarsely chopped
2 cloves garlic, peeled and sliced
1 cup chopped flat-leaf parsley, plus more for garnish
2 shallots, peeled and chopped
Pinch of nutmeg
1 slice bread, moistened with water and squeezed dry
Salt and freshly ground pepper

1 large roasting chicken, ready for stuffing (up to 3–4 pounds)
1 tablespoon soft butter
Gravy (made of flour, drippings, and chicken broth)

Heat the oil in a medium-sized *sauteuse* (deep pan). Add the onion and lightly sauté. Then add the sausage; sauté for a couple of minutes, stirring with a wooden spoon. Place the mixture in a large bowl and add the chestnuts, spinach, ham or salt pork, garlic, parsley, shallots, nutmeg, bread, and salt and pepper to taste. Blend the entire mixture thoroughly with either wooden spoons or your hands.

Stuff the bird with the mixture without packing it too tightly. Once all the openings are stuffed, sew and truss the chicken with cook's twine. Set it into a roasting pan, coat with the butter, and roast, covered, in a preheated 325°F oven for 1 hour.

Remove the cover and check for doneness. If it's done, return the chicken to the oven just until the skin is golden, then remove it and let it stand for 10 minutes.

Remove the stuffing, slice it into thick slabs, and layer into a casserole dish. Also cut the chicken into thick slices and place these, along with the legs and wings, on top.

Make a thin, but flavorful gravy from the pan drippings and drizzle it over the top. Sprinkle with parsley and serve.

CHAPTER FOUR

Potée Auvergnate
AND
Gâteau aux Noix

Potée Auvergnate
(Marie Chirade's Cabbage Soup with Chunks of Pork)
from the Auvergne Region

Marie Chirade stepped out onto the porch and waited for the two women. A withered hand patted a stray white curl back into place while the other hand smoothed the blue-checked apron over her wraith-like body. Her illness was ebbing, she told herself, and her strength was increasing. As she watched Sophie and Kate approach, a smile enveloped her face. Marie would make it through this day one way or another. It was too important.

"Sophie, it has been years," she said with a slight rasp to her voice. "You look so much like your mother. I see it there in your smile." Marie grasped Sophie's shoulders with a strength that surprised even her and placed a kiss on each cheek in greeting.

"*Merci,*" Sophie said as she stepped aside. "And this is my dear friend Kate. Kate Barrington. She knows a smattering of French."

Kate extended her hand. "Very pleased to meet you, Madame Chirade."

"How delightful to meet you too, and I know a smattering of English," Marie chirped as she ushered them inside. "And please, call me Marie."

The moment the front door opened, the pungent aroma of cabbage and savory pork immediately swept past Sophie. "Mmmm. It smells delicious in here and oh, so familiar. What are you cooking?" Sophie asked. The two women edged into the small hallway behind Marie.

"A local specialty, *Potée Auvergnate.* Since you consented to stay for lunch, I thought I would prepare something nice—something I used to make with your mother. Basically, it's just cabbage soup with chunks of pork. It's easy to make. Of course, during the war, we would pretend to have pork, but surely your mother prepared this for you in the past, *oui?*"

"*Oui!* But I guess I never realized where the recipe came from. Now that *Maman* has gone, I am beginning to realize how little I know about . . ." She stopped short.

—*A Cup of Redemption,* pages 64–65

Just then a timer went off in the kitchen. "I believe our *déjeuner* is ready," Marie said, avoiding [Sophie's] question. She stood and moved slowly toward the kitchen.

Sophie looked at Kate, shrugged, picked up the tray, and followed. Marie lifted the lid on the stew and once again the pleasant aroma, rich with the fragrances of garlic and salt pork, filled the room. Swimming in the thick broth were turnips, potatoes, carrots, leeks, and cabbage: a full and hearty meal. She ladled three bowls full and set them on the table.

—*A Cup of Redemption,* page 74

Every region, in fact every village, has its own specific ingredients for *potée,* but because Marie Chirade was hosting Sophie and Kate in the Auvergne, this is surely what she would have prepared.

3 pounds pork shoulder

1 ham knuckle and/or a Polish Kielbasa sausage

Unlimited carrots, peeled and cut into lengths of 6–8 inches

1 cabbage, cleaned and cut into 8 wedges

1 bouquet garni (thyme, laurel, and parsley tied with cook's twine)

1 onion, pierced all over with cloves

8–12 medium-sized potatoes, peeled and cut into quarters

4 turnips, peeled and cut into thick slices

1 large leek, well washed, white parts only, cut into slices

If the meat has been greatly salted, soak it overnight in cold water. In the morning, pour off the water, rinse the meat, and then replace it in a pot with fresh cold water. Bring to a boil, then turn the heat down and simmer for 1 1/2 hours. Add the carrots and cabbage and cook for 5 minutes, then add the bouquet garni and the onion. After 30 minutes, add the potatoes, turnips, and leek. Continue to simmer for another 45 minutes. Check for flavor and seasonings.

The broth itself can be served separately as one meal, and the sliced meat and vegetables served on a large platter as another meal. Be sure to pour the broth over the meat and vegetables or serve a small pitcher with the juices. This *potée* is a typical Auvergnate dish and dates back to ancient times.

Gâteau aux Noix
(Walnut and Honey Cake)
from the Auvergne Region

Their conversation remained light . . . about the weather, about farm prices, about what would become of farming now that France was biting down on another bullet of belt tightening. Nothing more about family until after they had finished lunch. Marie brought out a coffee cake, cut it, and turned to prepare coffee. Sophie poked the tines of her fork into the warm cinnamon-laced cake. She let the sticky goodness cross her tongue and she swooned.

—*A Cup of Redemption,* page 72

Cake

6 eggs, separated
1/2 cup local honey
Pinch of salt
1 teaspoon vanilla extract
1/2 teaspoon ground cinnamon
1 teaspoon vanilla extract
2/3 cup fine, light rye bread crumbs
2 cups walnuts, ground fine

Cream

1/3 cup honey
1 tablespoon espresso coffee
5 egg yolks
Pinch of salt
3/4 cup (1 1/2 sticks) unsalted butter, room temperature

Decoration

1/2 cup walnuts, ground fine
12 walnut halves

Cake

Preheat the oven to 325°F and butter two 9-inch cake pans. Flour the bottoms very lightly; shake out any excess.

Mix the egg yolks, honey, salt, cinnamon, and vanilla together. Using an electric mixer, beat until the mixture is light, extremely foamy, and forms a ribbon when lifted from the beaters. Whip the egg whites in a separate bowl until stiff. Mix one-quarter of their volume into the egg yolk mixture.

Mix together the bread crumbs and 2 cups of ground walnuts. Slide the remainder of the egg whites onto the yolks. Sprinkle the mixture with the bread crumbs and walnuts. Fold until all the ingredients are perfectly, albeit lightly, blended.

Turn half of the batter into each prepared pan and bake in the preheated oven for 35 to 40 minutes. Invert the layers on two cake racks and cool completely.

Cream

Bring the honey to a boil in a small pan. Add the coffee to the honey. Place the egg yolks in the small bowl of an electric mixer, add the salt, and whip until they start to foam. Pour the honey, without bothering to let it cool, in a steady stream into the egg yolks. Continue whipping until the mixture spins a heavy ribbon and is completely cold. Reduce the speed of the mixer and gradually add the butter to obtain a smooth buttercream.

ASSEMBLY

Fill the layers with one-third of the cream. Spread a thin layer of cream on the sides and top of the cake and apply the remaining ground walnuts all around the cake. Place the walnut halves around the outside edges of the cake and voilà! You are done!

This cake recipe has been adapted from another amazing French cookbook, called none other than *When French Women Cook* (pages 91–92), by the celebrated Madeleine M. Kamman.

CHAPTER FIVE

Tartine au Saindoux et Oignons
Artichauts Farcis Grand'mère
AND
Grand'mère's Potage

Tartine au Saindoux et Oignons
(Marcelle's Favorite Pork Lard Sandwich)
from the Brittany Region

Tomas's face suddenly appeared over her mother's shoulder. He leered at her in the way that she had come to despise. She determined to leave that very night. After a simple dinner of toasted bread with her favorite *saindoux,* she feigned sleep and slipped off to bed.

—*A Cup of Redemption,* pages 80–81

It has been said that *saindoux* is nothing more than pork fat or pork-flavored rendered lard. It was often used instead of butter in the early twentieth century and was also a substitute for butter during World War II. Well known as a "poverty food," it was cheap—yet for impoverished families it was pure satisfaction spread upon a single slice of bread. Imagine a somewhat liquefied substance the flavor of bacon glistening on the only piece of bread left for the family. For Marcelle as a young girl, this was not only a staple but a pure delight. No actual recipe will be provided. Imagine, instead, her joy!

Paris, 1940

> Marcelle purchased *Le Figaro* while Thierry handed several sticky francs to the tobacconist for a small paper cone filled with candy. As he carefully unwrapped the sweets, she opened the paper and read, "War is competing with eternal Paris. But springtime in our fair City, with war looming on the horizon, is like a lovely woman being forced to accept the attentions of a man she despises." Oh, didn't she know what that was like! Her eyes scanned for notices of ration cards available at city hall. Only bread tickets at first. Yes, she knew that. She looked for the date when full rationing would follow. She read the recipes on how best to use leftovers. She chuckled. Leftovers? What was that? The article described stuffing an artichoke. If only she had an artichoke. She laughed out loud now, and grabbed up Thierry's hand. He smiled up at her not knowing the joke as they walked into a *marché* to purchase a few items for their picnic.
>
> —*A Cup of Redemption,* page 90

The joke in this matter is that under no circumstances could Marcelle or anyone else in Paris find an artichoke. But a gal can dream, and that was what helped Marcelle handle the life of uncertainty as the Germans began their march on Paris.

Artichauts Farcis Grand'mère
(Grandmother's Stuffed Artichokes)
from the City of Paris

STEP ONE: PREPARING THE ARTICHOKES

4 artichokes

Trim the tips of the artichokes' leaves with scissors. To keep them compact, tie twine around the middle of each artichoke, then up and over it, and knot the cord underneath. Place the artichokes in a pot with water to cover, bring to a boil, and simmer 10 minutes. Take from the water and cool. Remove the center leaves and scrape out the fuzzy choke with a spoon, leaving a hollow space for the stuffing.

STEP TWO: PREPARING THE STUFFING

6 tablespoons (3/4 stick) sweet butter

2 tablespoons chopped onion

1 teaspoon chopped garlic

2 cups finely chopped leftover roasted meat (if you are so fortunate as to have any) such as lamb, beef, veal, or chicken

1/2 cup finely chopped boiled ham

1/2 cup finely chopped cooked smoked tongue

1 egg

1 tablespoon chopped parsley

1 teaspoon chopped chives

1 teaspoon salt

1 teaspoon white pepper

1/2 teaspoon *Épices Parisiennes* (mixture of cloves, rosemary, marjoram, paprika, mace, nutmeg, cinnamon, bay leaf, and sage; if this is not available, use equal parts dried rosemary, marjoram, bay leaf, and thyme)

1/4 cup cognac**

1/2 cup white bread crumbs

4 very thin slices larding pork, each 4 inches square

*During war years, any meat became acceptable—including pigeon, cat, or dog. It was all desperately needed protein, because the Germans were bent on starving the French. Period.

**Can you see this was a recipe women only dreamed of during the war? When asked what she ate during the War, Marcelle simply tossed back her head, laughed, and said, "We could always find a good bottle of Chateau Margaux!" But, the truth is . . . well, the truth is that wine was never available to her.

Melt the butter in a saucepan. When it's foaming, simmer the onion 4 minutes; do not brown. Add the garlic and cook 2 minutes; add leftover chopped meat and simmer 5 minutes. Add all the remaining ingredients, except the larding pork, and mix thoroughly. Check the seasoning. Divide this stuffing evenly to fill the hollowed artichokes. Tie a slice of larding pork on the top of each choke.

Step Three: Cooking the Stuffed Artichokes

4 stuffed artichokes 2 cups brown stock
1/2 cup dry white wine – (or water, if that is all you have)

Place the artichokes in a roasting pan and pour in the brown stock and white wine. Cover, bring to a boil on top of the stove, and place in a preheated 350°F oven for 1 hour or until the leaves pull off easily. Remove the twine and arrange the artichokes on a warm serving platter. Cook the sauce until it is reduced by half. Strain through a fine-mesh wire strainer and serve on the side.

—Re-created from *Antoine Gilly's Feast of France*, pages 287–88

Grand'mère's Potage
(Leek and Potato Soup)
from the Brittany Region

"You know what seems curious—almost eerie?" Marcelle asked Genévième. Her friend stared at her. How could she guess?

"There's no panic," Marcelle continued. "Only outrage. People are simply upset that this bombing in Paris has caused such a mess!"

"That's the French for you! Almost like these things couldn't possibly be happening. Hmm! Let's stop at the *marché* before going home. *J'ai faim!* When we get home you can prepare your *grand mere's potage.*"

"That seems so long ago, doesn't it?" Marcelle murmured.

—*A Cup of Redemption,* pages 100–01

Shred the white part of 2 leeks and lightly sauté in 2 tablespoons butter. Add 3 cups of potatoes cut into quarters. Moisten with a quart of white consommé. [Undoubtedly, water filled the bill here.] Season and boil fast. As soon as the potatoes are cooked, mash them and rub through a sieve. Lighten with a few tablespoons of consommé or cream and finish off with 1/4 cup of fresh butter and a tablespoon of chervil leaves.

Or if fate did not cooperate and
they were stuck with *topimbour*...

Puree of Jerusalem Artichoke Soup*

Peel and quarter 4 to 5 Jerusalem artichokes and cook them in white consommé (or water). Rub through a sieve and lighten with 2 cups of consommé. Bring to a boil, stir, and finish off by incorporating 1/4 cup (1/2 stick) of fresh butter. Serve with small croutons fried in butter.**

*Jerusalem artichoke is another name for *topimbour,* the dreaded but most likely vegetable available to Marcelle in Paris during the war.

**Now imagine the luxury of consommé and butter during the war years. But Marcelle had been raised in poverty and knew how to flourish. Once again, she added a bit of *saindoux* when all else failed.

FRANCE - WWII
North Sea
UNITED KINGDOM
NETHERLANDS
GERMANY
BELGIUM
LUXEMBOURG
English Channel
Albert
Ste. Barbe
Verdun
Metz
PARIS
Mont Saint-Michel
Vannes
OCCUPIED ZONE
SWITZ.
Fontanières
Clermont-Ferrand
Lyon
ATLANTIC OCEAN
Bordeaux
FREE ZONE
ITALY
MONACO
ANDORRA
Mediterranean Sea
SPAIN
N
0
100 mi
0
100 km

CHAPTER SIX

Soupe à l'Oignon Gratinée

Soupe a l'Oignon Gratinée
(Marcelle and André's French Onion Soup
with Grated Cheese)
from the City of Paris

Paris, August 1941

It had been a particularly strenuous workday, and usually Marcelle had no energy for anything or anyone. But for some reason, she started up a conversation with a young man in the line leading to the *marché* (market). As they both eased through the queue toward the food bins, they found that what they had come for was long gone. Just as they both reached for the last onion, their hands met. Electricity shot through Marcelle's body as they stood with their hands wrapped around each other's. Marcelle threw her head back, and her low, resonant laughter filled the now-empty aisles of the store. The young man released his grip as they both headed to check out. There was no more food left in the store. He handed the clerk his last ticket as the lowly onion was wrapped and handed to Marcelle. *L'amour des oignons!* Yes, it was a love of onions—or simply the need for food—that brought the two together.

—*A Cup of Redemption,* page 103

RECIPE:

1/2 cup or 1 stick sweet butter

4 cups thinly sliced Bermuda onions

1 clove garlic, finely chopped

2 tablespoons white flour

1 cup dry white wine

2 quarts of beef stock or beef broth

1 teaspoon salt

1/2 teaspoon black pepper

1/4 cup dry sherry

12 small slices dry French bread

1 cup grated Parmesan cheese

Melt the butter in a deep saucepan, add the onions, and cook for 10 minutes over a high flame until they brown. Lower the heat and add the garlic and flour; cook 3 minutes or until the flour is slightly brown. Add the wine, stock, salt, and pepper; simmer 30 minutes. Let the liquid reduce in volume to 6 large soup cups. Stir in the sherry. Check the seasoning.

Pour into ovenproof soup cups. Place two slices of the bread on top of each cup of soup and sprinkle the bread with grated cheese. Put under the broiler to brown before serving.

BELGIUM
LUX.
GERMANY
Thionville
Ste. Barbe
Verdun
Metz
Nancy
Alsace
Champagne-
Ardennes
Lorraine
Seine River
Burgundy
N
0
25 mi
0
25 km
Franche-
Comté
SWITZERLAND

CHAPTER SEVEN

Coquilles St. Jacques
Soupe au Lait
AND
Pot-au-Feu

Coquilles St. Jacques
(Michela's Sea Scallops)
from the Lorraine Region

As for the two siblings [Sophie and Julien], they reconnected like a well-practiced comedy team. Even though they were in weekly contact by phone or Internet, each time they came together they reveled in each other's company. Michela added a bit to the conversation, smiled, and headed into the kitchen to finish dinner.

"*Coquilles St. Jacques*," she finally announced. "In honor of my sister-in-law, Sophie, and her friend, Kate." She grinned.

"Ah, *ma chère*, my favorite too!" Julien jumped up and gave her a quick peck on her cheek. He then pulled Sophie to her feet.

"She prepares the freshest sea scallops," Sophie exclaimed to Kate. "They're incredible!" She smacked her lips together as they followed the tantalizing aroma to the dining room. Julien slowed to open another bottle of white wine and they all sat down at the table.

"So, what is your secret with your sea scallops, Michela?" Kate asked as she dipped her finger into the delicate sauce surrounding the scallops.

"Plenty of butter and freshly grated orange peel," was her reply. "It's probably the most French of all my cooking, as I usually follow my Italian heritage."

"Oh, you are in for some heavenly treats here, Kate." Sophie said kindly. "Our entire family has enjoyed your family's treasure trove of recipes, Michela."

—*A Cup of Redemption,* page 113

Serves 4

1 pound large sea scallops (2 cups sliced)
3/4 cup dry white wine
2 cups sliced fresh mushrooms
1/2 teaspoon salt
1/2 teaspoon pepper
1 bay leaf
2 tablespoons shallots, minced
3 tablespoons unsalted butter, plus more for dotting
1/4 cup flour
3/4 cup milk, plus more as needed
2 egg yolks
1/2 cup heavy whipping cream
1/2 teaspoon orange juice (optional)
1 tablespoon granulated sugar (optional)
3 tablespoons grated Swiss cheese
1 cup plain bread crumbs
Freshly grated orange peel

Tip: Some people like to soak the scallops first in 1 cup milk. (This will alleviate shrinkage while cooking.) Soak for at least an hour covered in milk in the refrigerator. Rinse them and pat dry before using.

Place the scallops in a saucepan with the wine, mushrooms, seasonings, and herbs. Add water, if necessary, to barely cover the ingredients. Bring the mixture to a simmer, then cover the pan and simmer slowly for 5 minutes. Remove the scallops and mushrooms, and place them into a bowl. Rapidly boil down the cooking liquid until it's reduced to 1 cup.

Melt 3 tablespoons of butter in a new pan and stir in the flour until smooth. Cook slowly for 2 minutes without browning. Remove the pan from the heat and beat in the scallop cooking liquid. Replace pan back on the stove and whisk over medium heat until the sauce thickens. Thin with the milk.

Blend the egg yolks in a bowl with half of the heavy cream. Beat in the hot scallop-liquid sauce driblets. Return the mixture to the pan. Cook over medium heat, stirring, until the sauce comes to a slight boil. Thin, as necessary, with more cream or milk. Carefully correct the seasonings. Add the orange juice and sugar if you like.

Fold two-thirds of the sauce into the scallop-and-mushroom mixture. Spoon into lightly buttered large scallop shells or individual ramekins (small round baking bowls). Spoon on the remaining sauce and sprinkle with the cheese. Top with bread crumbs and place little dabs of butter on top, then sprinkle with freshly grated orange peel. Place under the broiler until lightly browned. Serve with crusty bread, if desired.

Soupe au Lait
(Milk Soup)

"Oh, Julien, the sound was unmistakable: that swish-swish-swish of our father's corduroy work pants; the sound of his heavy boots hitting the back steps; the rancor in his voice as he swore at our neighbors. Why, I remember we—you, Gérard, and me—would look at each other and race for the stairs."

Julien nodded slowly as she continued.

"Just the cadence of Papa's footfalls taught us to detect his mood. '*Soupe au lait* is home,' Gérard used to say."

"What? What did he say?" Julien almost choked on the liqueur.

"'*Soupe au lait* is home.' The milk, which can sour at a second's notice, has arrived at our door. You remember."

"Gérard was a clever one, though. I remember one time when . . ."

"I remember," Sophie interrupted, "that most nights were no different than any other. Don't change the subject. We would grab our books and race up the stairs to take cover. Even the thought of him catching us reading sent us flying. You remember that, don't you?"

—*A Cup of Redemption,* page 115

Soupe au lait is a turn of phrase, just as Sophie explained, meaning that their father's mood could change so quickly there was little time to prepare for it. Why, even milk could take more time than he did to sour! Everyone had to be on their guard.

Pot-au-Feu
(Marcelle's Beef Stew)
from the Lorraine Region

> [Marcelle recounts:] I bent low to ease the stew from the oven. I can count on his not helping so I quickly wipe my tears on the pot holder. I heft the stoneware tureen to the table, which is filled with a small scrap of hard salt pork, a bit of leftover beef, and the now-burnt vegetables. The sausage that is called for in the recipe was not added, as the week's check was unusually small. Or so he tells me. But he tends to notice the omission of ingredients and blames me for my inept cooking. I prepare myself. My eyes mist over as I attempt to keep from crying. To my children, I must appear as if I am not offended, but I, too, have nowhere to hide. Guilt once again overwhelms me. The only life I have created for my children is in the ring closest to the eye of a storm. Eventually, and it is one of the few things we all can count on, the storm will come to rest on each one of us, one at a time. There is no rhyme or reason to it. It is just how he is. We constantly sit in dread.

—*A Cup of Redemption*, page 119

This type of stew is prepared by the country people all over France every Sunday because it's so versatile. On Sunday, the beef and vegetables are usually eaten. The broth is used as a consommé, a soup base, or an extension of one meal to the next. On the third day of the week, the few scraps of leftover beef are placed into a terrine, along with a bit of salt pork, splashed with the broth, and roasted in the oven with, hopefully, a few more vegetables thrown into the mix. If you are lucky, sausage has been added at one stage or another.

2 pounds beef shin, brisket, or shoulder
2 pounds beef knuckles or sausage
4 quarts cold water
6 carrots, peeled
4 white turnips, peeled
2 onions, stuck with 4 cloves each
1 bunch celery
1 parsnip, peeled
3 cloves garlic
2 leeks, white parts only
2 sprigs parsley
1 bay leaf
1 teaspoon dried thyme leaves
6 peppercorns
3 tablespoons salt

Place the beef and beef knuckles in a deep stockpot, cover with the cold water, and bring to a boil. Remove the scum that rises to the top. Add all the vegetables, herbs, and seasonings. Simmer, uncovered, 30 minutes; remove the vegetables and keep on the side. Continue to simmer the meat and bones, uncovered, 15 minutes more. Then cover and simmer for 2 hours or until the meat is tender, adding the vegetables back into the mixture to reheat. Strain and save the broth. Slice the meat and serve on a platter with the vegetables. This dish can be served with condiments, such as Dijon mustard, ketchup, or a horseradish sauce.

> [Kate tells of her own mother's Sunday culinary routine:] First, my mother would take a good-sized piece of chuck roast—the largest piece she could fit into the proper roasting pan—no, the only roasting pan. She placed a couple of tablespoons of Crisco into the roaster, popped the roast in and placed it on top of the stove where she seasoned the meat liberally with salt and pepper, and then seared the meat on both sides. She would then put it into a low oven to cook while we were all at church. When we returned, the redolent aroma of roasting meat filled the entire house and our appetites would swell with thoughts of this wonderful meal. Mom's roast beef, homemade mashed potatoes, and gravy were some of the best flavors to ever cross our family's tongues. We never had better.

But then the week would progress! On Monday night, Mom would chop up leftover meat and sauté it with potatoes and onions—lots of onions—and the flavor was still full—something we looked forward to. Unfortunately, it was Wednesday's meal that still haunts me! Nowhere in all my world travels have I ever been faced with a plate of grey-colored mush piled onto a plate, except with Wednesday's leftovers. To this day, I can't tell you what was left in those leftovers—other than the color of grey! With a family of seven, what else could have possibly been added? I don't want to know, either.

—*Savoring the Olde Ways**

**Savoring the Olde Ways* is part of a series of travel/food memoirs, yet to be published.

CHAPTER EIGHT

Polish Beef Lung

AND

Capelettes Farcis aux Epinards avec une Sauce Bolognaise

Polish Beef Lung
from the Champagne Region

Spring in Ste. Barbe, 1952

Sophie opened a side door to a dank stairwell, which led up the steep wooden steps to Mimi's grandmother's apartment.

Immediately, she was rocked by a sickly odor descending from above. *Mon Dieu! What is that awful smell?* As she stood on the stairs while attempting not to gag, the door opened from above and Mimi's bright face beamed down on her.

"Are you coming up? What took you so long?" she asked, bounding down the stairs to grab her friend's hand and drag her up the steps. White goose feathers hovered in their midst and clung to them on their ascent. Mimi's pigtails had been turned from blond to white before they reached the uppermost landing . . .

"What's happening?" Sophie asked. "And what is your *grand'mère* cooking?" She knew Mimi's Polish grandmother was especially poor. She was a widow and raised her own geese, rabbits, chicken, even turkeys for barter, but Sophie couldn't detect what the awful smell was.

"Oh, that's beef lung. Grand'mère was given a nice lung in exchange for all these feathers."

"Do you like lung?" Sophie squinched her nose up in disgust.

"It's okay, I guess. But then I eat anything." Mimi flipped her pigtails behind her.

"I've got an explosive idea," Sophie said in a loud whisper. "Today's the day we are going to learn to—to smoke!" She jumped back and shrieked with an eight-year-old's delight. "Do you have any money for cigarettes?"

—*A Cup of Redemption,* pages 127–28

I could find no Polish person who would divulge to me the precious recipe for beef lung. Well, maybe there is a reason. Maybe it's not so precious! So maybe that recipe wouldn't whet your appetite either.

In the little iron mining village of Ste. Barbe, there were many ethnicities living side by side. After World War II, men from all over Europe were in desperate need of work, so many flocked to Ste. Barbe, bringing their families with them. It was there that an entire generation became aware of foods and cultures beyond their own regional borders.

She shook her head to clear her mind and joined in with her brother as they repeated an old jingle they had made up as children: "Polish, French, Polish; Belgium, Italian, and once again, Italian . . ." They laughed together as they crossed the street. "French, Italian, Polish, Russian, and last but never least, French."

"What's that about?" Kate asked them.

"Oh, that's how we used to keep track of our diverse neighborhood. Miners and their families came from all Europe for work," Sophie replied.

"And that is why we have a varied and rich cuisine, right, Soph?" Julien said, licking his lips.

"Ah, yes, that's right. Remember we mentioned Michela's family coming from Italy? Her father moved here from Italy to work in the mines, and then he married into an Italian family here . . ."

—*A Cup of Redemption,* pages 132–33

Capelettes Farcis aux Epinards avec Une Sauce Bolognaise

(Jean-Pierre's Capelette with Spinach Filling and Bolognaise Sauce)

from the Champagne Region

Sophie and Julien's cousin Jean-Pierre—who, during childhood, lived a couple of doors away from them in Ste. Barbe—invited Sophie and Kate to his home in the Champagne region to teach Kate her first French culinary lesson: a family favorite, Capelette with Spinach Filling and Bolognaise Sauce. During Kate's tour of France, she found that many of the "traditional family recipes" she was taught were not French but actually Italian.

The next excerpt was also taken from a post in *Savoring the Olde Ways* blog. Jean-Pierre and his wife, Martine, have begun a culinary lesson.

> But first, the pasta! It was clear that Jean-Pierre and Martine had prepared this dish many times in the past. I [Kate] could see they had a good rhythm going and . . . into the kitchen we went . . . and back into the dining room where she immediately set about fluffing flour wildly onto a clean, plastic-coated tablecloth. He extended a cloth-covered board up the wall where it rested on the window ledge from the table . . . just to ensure plenty of space. Now the area for rolling out the pasta was perfect for them . . . a long and unobstructed space . . . something the tiny kitchen did not afford. Then he twisted a bit of dough out from under a cloth-covered bowl as she quickly covered the bowl again. He patted out the small chunk of dough . . . just enough to fit into the gleaming silver pasta maker that had been conveniently attached to the side of the table. Right down the center of the table went the flour action, and quickly a three-foot ribbon of dough, which had been cranked out of the little machine, snaked along the flour. In moments, back in came Martine, as if on cue, with the spinach filling. They worked like a synchronized team—a fluff of flour—a flick of the doughy ribbon—a cutting of four-inch squares—a plopping of spinach filling into the center—a quick folding over of each square to secure the mixture—and a pinching of the edges. "Nothing to it!" he said. And voilà! It was complete . . . well, actually it needed to rest and so did we.
>
> Once the *capelette* had been made, Jean-Pierre shifted into his role as host and the champagne began to flow. We moved into the living room—which was an extension of the dining area where the culinary arts had just been performed—and settled into comfortable seats. A fire crackled lively in the fireplace and the TV, which was turned on to an English-speaking station, appeared to be turned on for my benefit. (They spoke very little English.)
>
> As Martine bustled about in the kitchen, Jean-Pierre put down his glass of champagne and walked over to the fireplace mantel where an antique brass lamp sat in an honored

position. "This," he said, "was my father's own mining lamp—the light he carried with him every day throughout all the thirty years he worked the iron mines. It was very difficult work. They worked hard and for very long hours each day . . . and this light . . ."

His voice cracked with emotion. "I guess this lamp represents more than just light to me. It represents my father . . . who he was . . . the hard work he endured . . . the home and security he provided his family . . . and the love he showed us children."

Sophie turned to him and smiled warmly. "Yes, I loved your father so much—almost more than my own." Her family story was beginning to be told.

—*Savoring the Olde Ways*

Spinach Filling

1 pound fresh spinach
1 pound ricotta
2 tablespoons heavy cream
4 tablespoons freshly grated *Parmigiano Reggiano* cheese
1/4 teaspoon nutmeg
Pinch black pepper
1 tablespoon salt
1 egg

In a pot of boiling water, cook the spinach with half of the salt until tender; about 3 minutes. Remove the spinach from the boiling water and let cool for 2 to 3 minutes. Squeeze out the water from the spinach and chop it up roughly. In a mixing bowl, combine chopped spinach, ricotta, egg, heavy cream, and 4 tablespoons *Parmigiano Reggiano*. Season with the nutmeg, remaining salt, and black pepper.

Capelette Dough

2 cups unbleached all-purpose flour
3 large eggs, lightly beaten
1 tablespoon olive oil (optional)

Sift the flour onto a clean work surface and make a well in the center. Pour the beaten eggs into the well. With a fork, mix the flour and eggs together until the dough is soft and begins to stick together, about 3 minutes. When the dough forms a mass, transfer it to a slightly floured clean surface and knead until satiny and resilient, about 10 to 15 minutes. Cover with a clean cloth and set aside for an hour.

Roll the rested dough through the pasta-making machine, creating a ribbon 3 feet long and about 5 inches wide. Cut the dough into squares. Top each square with a tablespoonful of the spinach filling, fold the dough over to trap the filling, pinch the edges, and let set covered with a kitchen towel until you've prepared all of the *capelettes*. Cook in salted boiling water. They are ready when they come to the surface of the water—about 2 minutes. Serve with Bolognaise Sauce and freshly grated Parmesan cheese.

Bolognaise Sauce

3 tablespoons Extra Virgin Olive Oil
1 chopped small onion
1 clove garlic
2 pounds of very lean ground beef
1 cup red wine
1/2 cup beef broth
1 can (28-ounce) Imported Crushed Tomatoes
A pinch of fresh basil, sage, and rosemary
1 bay leaf
Salt and pepper
3 sugar cubes

In a large sauteuse (frying pan), sauté the beef, onion, and garlic in the olive oil.

Add basil, salt, pepper, 1 cup of red wine, and 3 sugar cubes (to eliminate the tomatoes' acidity). Add salt and pepper to taste. Stew over low heat for 2 hours. The more you cook the tomatoes, the less acidic your sauce will be. Jean-Pierre's Italian friends say that the Bolognaise Sauce is done when the fat comes back to the surface. (Spoon off excess fat before serving.)

To serve, pile the *capelettes* onto a heated platter, smother in the hearty Italian sauce—and shout, "*Viva la France!*"

CHAPTER NINE

Champagne
AND
Terrine aux Herbes

Champagne

Sophie's mouth was dry. She walked over to the sink to rinse out her coffee cup, filled it with water, and leaned against the sink as she drank it down in one gulp.

"I know I've put you into an awkward position," she said to Julien, then swiped the back of her hand across her mouth. "Kate, too, for that matter. I know you didn't want me to involve her, but she's the only one who isn't a family member, who can give me perspective. But I also need your help. When did you say Michela is due home?"

"She won't be home for a few hours." Julien said. He felt completely drained. He walked to the refrigerator, pulled out a bottle of champagne, popped the cork, and poured two flutes of the foamy essence. He turned and encouraged Sophie to join him back at the table. Drying her cup, she took the glass and toasted, "To *Maman*! God love you, dear *Maman*! *Tchin-tchin!*"

—*A Cup of Redemption,* pages 145–46

No recipe for champagne could possibly be given; they'd have to kill me for revealing their secrets.

Terrine aux Herbes
(Sophie's Baked Potted Meats)
from the Lorraine Region

Often hors d'oeuvres are served with champagne. *Pâté de foie gras* is one marvelous specialty and, indeed, was served that same evening before the *capelettes.* In France, this is easily purchased, so I won't include a recipe here. On another occasion, Kate was given a savory little morsel, a bit of cod liver on crostini. It too was quite delectable, but it also came straight from a can. No recipe necessary.

One of the favorite hors d'oeuvres Kate and Sophie were served, however, was *Terrine aux Herbes.* Sliced and paired with Riesling or champagne, it was always a delicate and flavorful first course. This country *pâté* of veal, ham, chicken livers, herbs, garlic, and wine is most often a traditional family recipe. Each family across France has different primary ingredients.

The difference between a *pâté* and a *terrine* is that the *pâté* is usually baked *en croûte* or in pastry. A *terrine* is baked in a porcelain crock and often served from same.

Serves 10

8 ounces fresh chicken livers

Flour

1 tablespoon butter

2 tablespoons vegetable oil

1 1/2 pounds lean veal, lean pork, and boiled ham, each coarsely ground then mixed (about 4 cups of the mixture)

1 tablespoon dried thyme or savory

4 cloves garlic, peeled and crushed

2 onions, peeled and hand-chopped

1 tablespoon mixed red, green, and black peppercorns

3 eggs

1 teaspoon of juniper berries

1 cup dry white wine

2 tablespoons port

1/2 cup chopped parsley

A few strips *saindoux* or lard back

2 x 1/2-inch slices cured ham or prosciutto

4 bay leaves

Trim the chicken livers; rinse and pat dry. Dredge in flour. Heat the butter and oil in a 9-inch skillet and sauté the livers on all sides for 2 minutes. Remove from the heat and set aside.

Add the chopped meats to the pan and mix with a wooden spoon. Add the herbs, garlic, onions, peppercorns, eggs, and juniper berries, continuing to mix well. Stir in the livers, wine, port, and parsley; cook for a few minutes. Preheat the oven to 350°F.

Line the bottom and sides of a terrine with half the slices of *saindoux* or lard back. Put one-third of the cooked stuffing in the bottom of the terrine. Place the strips of ham or prosciutto on top of the mixture and press down. Repeat these layers twice, pressing down with your hand to compress everything into the pan. Place the bay leaves on top along with the remaining lard back.

Put a sheet of aluminum foil over the top of the terrine, then the terrine lid. Place the terrine into a pan in the oven with enough hot water to come halfway up the terrine. Bake for 2 hours. Remove the foil (replacing the lid) and bake for an additional 15 minutes.

After taking the terrine out of the oven, remove the lid. Place a wooden board on top of the terrine weighted down with two or three cans of vegetables. Let cool. When cool, place in the refrigerator but keep the weight on the terrine to keep it compressed.

To serve the terrine, slice it down the middle then into uniform slices. Use a small spatula to remove slices from the terrine and onto individual plates. Serve with gherkins and French bread.

—Adapted from *The French Family Feast* by Mireille Johnston, pages 73–75

CHAPTER TEN

Ravioli Farcis au Cresson

Ravioli Farcis au Cresson
(Julien's World-Class Watercress Ravioli)
from the Lorraine Region

Lorraine, 2001

After she hung up the phone, Kate lay on the bed and thought about her conversation with her sister. She knew she was just awakening to the pain and anguish she had long ago submerged. Downstairs, she heard the faint strains of Sophie and Julien's laughter and the clattering of pots. Kate pushed the covers away from her and stood to go downstairs. She had faced enough for one day, and the promise of learning a "new" recipe—world-class watercress ravioli—compelled her to race down the stairs to join her friends.

—*A Cup of Redemption,* page 161

Pasta

2 1/2 cups flour
3 eggs
Pinch of salt

Mix the ingredients well to form a dough. Place the dough into a pasta machine and form into flat sheets. For more detail, see the recipe for Jean-Pierre's capelettes in Chapter Eight. Julien and Jean-Pierre are cousins, so they learned the same recipes.

Watercress Filling

2 minced shallots

1 tablespoon butter

1 1/2 cups de-stemmed watercress, divided

1 cup ricotta

1 ounce freshly grated *Parmigiano Reggiano* cheese

2 sage leaves, chopped

Salt and pepper to taste

2/3 cup whipping cream

2 tablespoons olive oil

Cook the shallots in the butter slowly until they're lightly browned. Add 1 cup of the watercress and let the mixture cool. Add the cheeses, sage, salt, and pepper. Mix well and place 1 tablespoon of the filling to each ravioli square. Brush the edges of the dough with a bit of water, then press together with tines of a fork. Boil for 4 minutes in boiling salted water. Remove with a slotted spoon onto a heated platter.

In a medium-sized sauce pan, and on a low flame, heat the cream, olive oil, plus more salt and pepper to taste. Add the remaining 1/2 cup of watercress. Mix quickly—15 seconds—and pour over the ravioli. Enjoy!

CHAPTER ELEVEN

Gâteau Nancy à la Crème Anglaise
AND
Boudin Blanc

Gâteau Nancy à la Crème Anglaise
(Chocolate and Grand Marnier Cake)
from the Lorraine Region

Lorraine, 2001

Yes, Sophie," said Annie as she and Kate returned to the living room bearing a *Gâteau Nancy,* a chocolate and Grand Marnier soufflé-type cake. "Your mother was a very good woman, a very resilient woman."

Sophie looked over at Annie and thought, *'Very resilient.' That's an interesting choice of words.*

Yvon jumped up and helped Kate with the four cake plates, forks, and a bowl of *Crème Anglaise,* placing it on the coffee table as Annie slid onto the settee. Her energy was spent.

"Would you do the honors, Sophie?" Yvon asked. "You have provided us with some luxurious treats."

"Yes, Sophie, we won't have to eat for a week."

"Certainly." Sophie stood and lifted the cake knife. "I didn't realize you both knew my mother—so well. I knew you, Yvon, grew up in the same village as my father, but my mother?"

"Oh, but of course we knew her. Maybe more so after you moved away from Ste. Barbe, but we lived in small communities."

"Actually, now that both my parents have gone, I've been trying to understand them," Sophie blurted out. "I can't believe I've waited until now." She leaned over the *gâteau,* made precise incisions, and lifted four equal pieces onto plates Kate was holding. Kate ladled a spoonful of the *Crème Anglaise* sauce over each slice and handed the cake around.

"It's not so odd, Sophie," said Yvon, gently. "We usually don't think to ask questions of our parents, or challenge them about their pasts. But that doesn't mean we ever stop wondering—wondering if who we are is part of who they were. *C'est normal.*"

"Did either of you ask your parents questions about their pasts?" Sophie asked.

Yvon took a bite of cake and his eyes smiled as he swallowed. "Mmm, this is marvelous! But heavens, no! What my parents' lives were like before I was born? Well, I guess the only way I found out was from overheard gossip, like the story of my father's broken rib. Anything that might have brought him shame or embarrassment, we never discussed. It was only because he was near Annie's grandmother's home that I was told about it later. Never at home."

—*A Cup of Redemption,* pages 174–75

. . . Picking up her fork, Annie began to eat. "Mmm. This *Gâteau Nancy* is quite delicious. I haven't had this in years. Do you have this recipe?" she rattled.

Sophie and Kate looked at each other. Clearly the door on this conversation had just slammed shut.

"No, Annie, I don't have the recipe. I bought it at a patisserie down the road from you." Sophie took her first bite of the bittersweet chocolate cake and almost swooned. "Mmm. This *is* good! I haven't had this since I was a kid."

—*A Cup of Redemption,* page 176

Gâteau Nancy is a specialty cake from the Lorraine region of eastern France where Sophie was raised. It contains no flour. Instead, its body and soft, dense texture come from ground almonds and grated chocolate. The small bits of chocolate retain their shape during baking and produce tiny pockets of dense chocolate flavor. The addition of a splash of Grand Marnier certainly can't hurt. Be sure to use a medium-sized springform cake pan.

SERVES 6–8

1/2 cup (1 stick) plus 1 tablespoon butter
4 1/2 ounces chocolate

4 eggs, separated
2/3 cup sugar
3 1/2 ounces almonds, finely ground
1–2 tablespoons Grand Marnier
1–2 tablespoons potato starch

Melt the butter in a double boiler, then clarify and set aside. Grate the chocolate and set aside.

In a large bowl, mix together the egg yolks and sugar, then add the almond powder and clarified butter. Gently stir in the grated chocolate and Grand Marnier.

Beat the egg whites until firm, then gently fold them into the batter. Finally, sift the potato starch over the batter and stir in very gently.

Pour the batter into a buttered and dusted springform cake pan and bake at 350°F for 40 minutes or until done. Serve with the following *Crème Anglaise.*

Crème Anglaise

This is a simple yet elegant custard sauce that's easily prepared—as long as you don't overcook it or allow it to curdle. One recommended method to prevent this is to prepare a cold-water bath and set it near the stove before you even begin.

2 cups half-and-half or whole milk
1 vanilla bean, split lengthwise
1/2 cup sugar
4 large egg yolks, room temperature

Set a large fine-mesh strainer over a medium bowl and set the bowl in a shallow pan of cold water.

In a large saucepan, combine the half-and-half and vanilla bean. Cook over moderately low heat just until small bubbles appear around the rim, about 5 minutes.

In another medium-sized bowl, whisk the sugar and egg yolks just until combined. Whisk in half of the hot half-and-half in a thin stream. Pour the mixture into the saucepan and cook over moderate heat, stirring constantly with a wooden spoon, until the sauce has thickened slightly, 4 to 5 minutes. Immediately strain the sauce into the bowl in the cold-water bath to stop the cooking. Scrape the vanilla seeds into the sauce. Serve right away or refrigerate until chilled. And, in this case, drizzle it over the *Gâteau Nancy.*

—Adapted from ChocoParis.com and *Modes de Paris: La Cuisine Régionale*

Boudin Blanc
(Jules' White Sausage Dinner)
from the Lorraine Region

Another Lorraine regional specialty is a holiday dish called *Boudin Blanc.* This is most often prepared for Christmas dinner, and was a favorite of Sophie and Julien's as they grew up. Prepared by their father, this was similar to black pudding (blood pudding) sausages, these are white pudding sausages made of pork, chicken, and plenty of onions. Oh, and if available, black truffle.

1/2 cup finely chopped onions
1/3 cup *saindoux* (melted lard)
1 1/2 cups soft bread crumbs
2 cups milk
1 1/2 pounds finely ground pork
3/4 pound finely chopped white poultry meat
2 cups cream
4 eggs
Salt, pepper, and nutmeg to taste
Shaved black truffles* (optional)
1/2 cup *panne fraîche* (fresh fat from the pig)

Cook the finely chopped onions in melted lard until nicely golden. Soak the bread crumbs in milk and let the mixture dry out near a low heat source to obtain a thick paste. Add the pork and chicken to the paste, along with the onions, cream, and whole eggs. Season with plenty of salt, pepper, and nutmeg.

Push the mixture into a cleaned intestine. Cook in a water bath for about 30 minutes. As the sausages float to the top, prick them with a pin to let the air out. Drain. Cover with a thick white cloth to keep "very white" and let them cool down.

Serve with a fresh *foie gras*** (sautéed 1 minute on each side) along with apples cooked in cognac and butter. Marvelous treat! Rich beyond belief, but then it is Christmas!

*Make sure they are *black* truffles—people will think that you are tricking them if they can't see the black specks in their sausage.

**Fresh foie gras is exactly that: fresh goose liver. *Pâté de foie gras* is goose liver mixed with many other ingredients and packed and baked in a terrine, as in the recipe for *Terrine aux Herbes* in Chapter Nine.

CHAPTER TWELVE

An Alsatian Detour: Baekheofe
AND
Hammeles

Baekheofe
(Christine's Baked Terrine of Lamb, Beef, and Pork)
from the Alsace Region

Due to the fact that Chapter 12 in *A Cup of Redemption* was a difficult time for each of the characters, very little time was given to the enjoyment of foods. Plus, rather than heading off to the Alsace as Sophie had told her brother, Julien, they headed off toward Paris. Little did Kate realize that an entire Alsatian specialty was being prepared for them by Sophie's dear friend Christine. Living just north of Strasbourg, Christine and her husband, Henri, are die-hard Alsatians who embrace all the traditional values handed down to them from their families. Fortunately, on a subsequent trip Kate is introduced to this couple and to the culinary delights of the Alsace. As an introduction, I will begin with a poem of which I attribute to the late Alsatian poet, George Spetz, who wrote of similar sentiments in his poem called, '*Poeme Gastronomique*'.

I, too, follow my grandmother's wisdom
Of simple, humble yet healthy foods.
I choose not the 'haute cuisine' of rich sauces,
But the 'cuisine pauvre' she shared with us.
All recipes were prepared with care; and
As they were handed down through the generations,
I find them now tucked within each recipe I prepare
A measure of memory, laughter, family, and love.

The following is an excerpt from the travel/food blog *Savoring the Olde Ways* regarding a visit to Alsace:

> "I remember when I was growing up," Christine began once again, "every Monday we would help our mother with the laundry (*lavoir*). This is where the ladies would all come with their baskets of laundry and buckets of water from the nearby stream, and we would wash our clothes together. After washing the clothes, we would struggle to twist them dry, and take them home. At home, we would put them on the lines to dry. So on that day, the lady of the house, or my mother, would take out all of the leftover rabbit from the refrigerator, add some vegetables, place it in a pot and cover it with a pastry topping and seal it, then take it to the bakery. There the baker would bake the dish, and she would pick it up after she had completed her laundry. This was the older version of *baekeofe.*
>
> "But nowadays, people make *baekeofe* in a manner that costs a lot of money. They use better cuts of meat like lamb and they add expensive wines. Oh, it is very different than the special dish of my youth, but it is equally good. So when we get home this evening, the entire meal will be waiting for us!"
>
> —*Savoring the Olde Ways*

Baekeofe is an Alsatian specialty made with cut-up lamb, beef, and pork. The meat is first marinated in white Riesling wine all night or 24 hours along with garlic, thyme, cloves, salt, and pepper. Peel potatoes and cut into six slices each. In a terrine, layer goose fat, then potato slices, meat, then onion, carrots, and leeks until all your meat and vegetables are layered together. End with a pear on top. Add wine to the top and possibly pigs' feet before sealing. Seal the lid into place with a paste of flour and water. Bake for 2 to 3 hours in a low oven.

Hammeles
(Lamb-Shaped Cake for Easter)
from the Alsace Region

Christine continued sharing some of the many traditions she learned as she was growing up:

"I'm a chocoholic, so I guess my favorite holiday would have to be Easter. You see, I came from a family of six children, and I was the youngest. My parents, for Easter, would prepare a large nest in the yard with colored eggs and chocolate eggs. I loved chocolate so much that I would sometimes steal the chocolate eggs from my brothers and sisters." A mischievous smile crept across her face at the thought of it. "Also, in the nest were new clothes, which were very important at Easter. But not just for Easter, as these were our special clothes for the entire year. Our old clothes were used for after school, or for play. Rarely were they handed down because they were in pretty bad shape each year, and because I was the youngest, there was no one to hand them down to anyway!

"I also remember that we would have a special cake for the Easter season which was called the *Hammele*. It is a lamb-shaped cake. You will probably see *Hammeles* in all of the bakeries or in the stores in Alsace during this time of year. Easter has just now passed but, perhaps, you noticed some of the cakes already. I have a form that I use to bake my own *Hammele*." She rushed into the kitchen to bring out the ceramic lamb-shaped form. In her hands were two pieces—equal lamb halves—with a metal clamp to hold it together while baking. The recipe for the cake is called a *Biscuit de Savoie* or the Savoy Sponge Cake.

—*Savoring the Olde Ways*

2 cups fine sugar
1 tablespoon vanilla-flavored sugar
or 1 teaspoon vanilla extract
1 cup plus 2 tablespoons potato flour
14 egg yolks
1 1/2 cups sifted flour
14 stiffly beaten egg whites

Cream the fine sugar and the yolks in a bowl until the mixture forms a ribbon. Add the vanilla-flavored sugar, flour, and potato flour mixed. At the last moment, fold in the stiff egg whites.

Put the mixture into a Savoy pan, or into a *Hammele* cake form that has been buttered and dusted with flour. Fill it only two-thirds full, and bake in a low oven of 325°F for one hour.

—Recipes adapted from Christine

CHAPTER THIRTEEN

Quiche Lorraine

Quiche Lorraine
(Sophie's Egg, Cheese, and Bacon Tart)
from the Lorraine Region

Hints of sunlight sparkled off the wet stones of Verdun, while along the river cries arose from a sculling team as it glided beneath [the bridge they stood on]. On the opposite shore, a large grey tour boat awaited business from tourists who, like Kate, were caught up in the history of Verdun.

"*Déjeuner, s'il vous plaît?*" asked Sophie.

"*Mais oui, madame. Merci beaucoup!*"

Linking arms, the two walked away from the river, where they spotted a small café. Hidden behind white lace curtains was a small, dark, but cozy room, which exuded the warmth they needed. They found a booth and slid in.

"Do you think we should try *Quiche Lorraine*. We are still in the Lorraine, aren't we?" Kate asked.

"We are, and we should. Good idea! *Quiche Lorraine pour deux!*"

Their eyes surveyed the contents of the serving case, where rather limp-looking salads stared back at them. And the quiche?

"Once those are microwaved, they will probably be rubbery, at best. What do you think?" The two women stared at the case, and then burst out laughing. This was not exactly what they had in mind, but for the time being, it would do. After Sophie promised to give Kate a real recipe for *Quiche Lorraine*, they opted for wine instead of coffee and settled into their seats.

Sophie leaned forward and rested her elbows on the table . . . [They continue their nonstop conversations as they wait for their lunch.]

—*A Cup of Redemption,* page 213

The sounds of a deluge reverberated through a nearby window. Sophie pulled her coat over her shoulders as stiffness ran through her back. The cold, damp air edged into her bones. She snugged the coat more closely about her.

"Wait, have we ordered yet?" Kate asked. The two giggled at their realization.

Sophie got up and ordered their food, and returned with two glasses of wine. "I'm starting to realize how little I know about your life, Kate."

Kate laughed at that. "Here I've been thinking that you have been keeping your feelings rather close to the vest, and I imagine I have been doing the same." She shrugged. "Probably I've been hiding behind the protective mantle of my old job." Kate paused. "Do we have time to order a carafe of wine?"

"*Oui!* Great idea!" Sophie said as she signaled the attention of the waitress. She quickly placed the order and in moments the carafe appeared with two wilted salads and two steaming-hot wedges of rubbery quiche.

Kate took a slow sip of wine. "Mmm. *Délicieux!*" She raised her glass to Sophie, and Sophie, in turn, raised hers. "Love and war; war and love. They can make you do strange and crazy things," Kate said, remembering some words her mother used to say. "And I certainly found that out on my own."

—*A Cup of Redemption,* pages 214–15

Step One: Dough

1 1/3 cups white flour
1 teaspoon salt
1/4 cup (1/2 stick) butter, cut into small chunks
1/4 cup lard, cut into small chunks
3 tablespoons cold water

Place the flour in a bowl and sprinkle with the salt. Then cut in the butter and lard and mix with your fingertips. Blend in the water and knead the dough only until it is well mixed. This dough should be prepared about 12 hours ahead of time and refrigerated, covered with cheesecloth.

When you're ready to make the quiche, roll the dough 1/4 inch thick and use it to line a 10-inch pie plate. Prick the bottom with a fork in several places and squeeze the edges of the tart as you would for a pie.

STEP TWO: FILLING

1/4 pound bacon, cut in 1-inch squares, lightly fried, and drained on paper toweling
2 cups heavy cream
3 eggs plus 3 egg yolks
1 1/2 teaspoons salt
1/4 teaspoon cayenne pepper
1/2 cup chopped chives

Spread the fried bacon bits on the bottom of the pastry shell. Beat the cream with the whole eggs and egg yolks, salt, and cayenne. Pour this liquid over the bacon to fill the crust. Sprinkle the chives over and place in a preheated 400°F oven for 20 minutes, or until the quiche rises and the top browns. Serve warm with a crisp (not limp) salad.

—Recipe adapted from *Antoine Gilly's Feast of France*, page 19

CHAPTER FOURTEEN

Biscuits au Citron
Crêpes
Fricassée de Poulet de Bresse à la Crème
AND
Chapon Sauté à l'Estragon

Biscuits au Citron
(Lemon Almond Cookies)
from the City of Paris

Paris, 2002

After seven sneezes, [Kate] mumbled, "I'm sorry. I have allergies, but maybe the worst is over." She daubed her eyes with a tissue, but found a place to sit on a padded rocker near the only open window. Madeleine and Sophie nodded in her direction, but quickly picked up their conversation. Madeleine, who had been awaiting their arrival, poured cups of hot tea and served a plate of [lemon] biscuits for the occasion. Like a small bird, she flitted about the room, then finally shut off the TV and sat down on the well-worn sofa beside Sophie.

Kate looked around. The five cats must have taken offense at her sneezes, for they had disappeared. The walls above Madeleine and Sophie were covered in photographs. Kate looked for someone she might recognize, but saw no one. She sat quietly tuning into an occasional French phrase, but almost dozed off.

"I'm so very glad you came to visit, Sophie," Madeleine began. "It has been years since you were last here, but my mother always spoke well of your mother and all of you. I believe they were close at one time . . . But I wouldn't know when that would have been." Her thin forefinger touched and retouched her bony chin.

—*A Cup of Redemption,* page 225

1/4 cup fine sugar
2 eggs, separated
Grated rind of 1 lemon
1/4 cup sifted flour
2 tablespoon potato starch
1 teaspoon ground almonds
Confectioners' sugar, for sprinkling

Add the fine sugar to a medium bowl along with the egg yolks; cream together until the mixture is firm. Add the lemon rind and mix with a wooden spoon. Add the sifted flour and the potato starch, along with the ground almonds. Whisk the 2 egg whites until they form a stiff froth and add to the bowl.

Pipe the mixture through a pastry bag into macaroon shapes 1 1/4 inches apart on a parchment-paper-lined cookie sheet. Sprinkle with confectioners' sugar and put into a slow oven (325°F) until light brown, about 12 minutes. Let the biscuits cool, then detach them and store them in a cookie jar—or in this case, a biscuit tin. Or serve immediately with tea or coffee.

Crêpes
from the Brittany Region

Sophie hesitated and then dove in. "That's one of the reasons for my visit. Now that she is gone I realize how little I know about her side of the family."

Madeleine nodded. "I was maybe five or six when our Grandmother Marie-Anne passed away, but I remember visiting her home when your mother was still living there. I remember homemade jams slathered on hot-from-the-griddle crêpes, along with her laughter and plenty of hugs." A wistful expression swept across her face, but lasted only a moment. She blinked.

Sophie turned to Kate, smiling broadly, "She's telling me of visiting my great-grandmother's house and how she loved the crêpes. As you've said before, dear Kate, memories are always wrapped around food."

—*A Cup of Redemption,* pages 225–26

The recipe for crêpes can be found in Chapter One. This is another connection between the family and a favorite food from the past.

Fricassée de Poulet de Bresse à la Crème
(Chicken Fricassee)
from the City of Paris

"Well, here's to finally finding answers for your mother, Sophie," Kate said, raising her glass in a toast. Kate clinked her glass with Sophie's and slowly sipped her wine as she waited for Sophie to continue. Finally, she asked, "So what does the rest of the letter say?"

Again, the waiter appeared and placed two separate plates of chicken before them. Kate tucked into her plate of chicken fricassee as Sophie began to play with her *Chapon Sauté à l'Estragon.*

"Aren't you hungry, Sophie?" Kate asked as she stuffed a bite of fricassee into her mouth.

—*A Cup of Redemption,* pages 230–31

The chickens that hail from the ancient area of Bresse are well known throughout the world for their incomparable quality and flavor. Poets over the centuries have been known to eulogize this specialty in both song and verse.

1 oven-ready Bresse chicken
Freshly ground salt and pepper
3 1/2 ounces pearl onions
2 teaspoons sugar
1/4 cup (1/2 stick) butter, divided
1 cup Chardonnay
9 ounces fresh mushrooms
2 cups *crème fraîche*

Divide the chicken into eight pieces. In a braising saucepan, lightly brown all the pieces in 2 tablespoons of the butter. Salt and pepper the chicken pieces liberally. Pour in the wine and add 2 cups of water. Cover the pan and braise for 20 minutes.

Meanwhile, peel the onions and clean the mushrooms by cutting off the stalks. (Save for another recipe.) Toss the onions and mushrooms in a small braising saucepan over low heat, using the remaining 2 tablespoons of butter. Five minutes before serving, sprinkle the sugar on top, glazing them, and then add salt to taste.

Remove the chicken pieces from the saucepan and put them aside on a warm platter. Reduce the liquid to half, then pour in the crème fraîche. Reduce again, then pour the sauce over the meat. Use the glazed onions and mushrooms as a garnish.

—Adapted from *Culinaria France* (1998), page 218

Chapon Sauté à l'Estragon
(Sautéed Capon with Tarragon Sauce)
from the City of Paris

A capon is young cock that has been castrated (can't imagine that as a job description) and fattened up.

Cut the capon into eight pieces and sauté in a pan with 2 to 3 tablespoons of butter. Cover and let the capon simmer on low heat until cooked completely. Remove the pieces and place on a warmed platter. Add a handful of crushed tarragon leaves and 1/2 cup of white wine to the meat juices in the sauté pan. Stir slowly, as you add some thickened veal gravy and heat through. Serve the tarragon gravy alongside each piece of capon.

CHAPTER FIFTEEN

Coq à la Bière
Potjevleesch
AND
Agneau Pré-Salé

Nord/Pas-de-Calais Region, 2001

Walking through the beveled-glass doors, they found themselves in a small but well-appointed lobby. The front desk was tucked into a side alcove decorated with Victorian-print wallpaper and brass lamps lending warmth to a small table. A handful of brochures advertising local businesses were fanned out, including several brochures listing tours of World War I battlegrounds. Sophie scooped up several and caught up with Kate, who had disappeared around a corner.

Tantalized by the spicy aroma of grilled sausages and onions, along with the bitter smell of hops and beer, Kate had followed her nose and ears to find friendly voices and a buzz of activity. Entering the dining area, they found it to be a warm, comfortable-looking brewpub. Beer mugs lined the shelves above the bar, and two bar maids feverishly drew frothy steins of beer and slid them along the counter. The two women were shown to their seats, where they slipped into a cushioned banquette.

The menu was one of charcuterie: *Andouillette* sausages, *coq à la bière,* and *potje vleesch.* Sophie gave Kate a quick tutorial on two of the Flemish-style foods. "*Coq à la bière* is a rooster who has seen better days but has given his life to be boiled in ale. And *potje vleesch* is made up of the lives of chicken, rabbit, and veal mixed together, and suspended in death in fatty jelly made with bones, plus onions and herbs."

"On that note," Kate said, "I'll follow your lead and order *Andouillette* sausages, *s'il vous plaît.*"

Once the daily specials had been ordered, Sophie requested the *pièce de résistance*: the house-made beer. She sank further into the banquette and said, "Ah, more than wine, I love my beer!"

—*A Cup of Redemption,* pages 248–49

Coq à la Bière
(Chicken Braised in Beer)
from the Nord/Pas-de-Calais Region
(the French border nearest to Flanders)

2 tablespoons olive oil, plus more as needed
1 large chicken cut into 8 pieces, fat removed
Freshly ground salt and black pepper
1 large onion, cut into medium slices
4 cloves garlic, roughly chopped
2 tablespoons white flour
4 cups dark beer—Belgian, if available
1 bouquet garni (5 parsley stems, 3 bay leaves, 2 green leek leaves, 12 sprigs fresh thyme, tied together, in cheesecloth if desired)

Heat 2 tablespoons of the oil in a large, heavy skillet over medium-high heat until it is hot but not smoking. Carefully add the chicken pieces, season them with salt and pepper, and cook on one side until the skin turns an even golden-brown, about 5 minutes. (Do not crowd the pan; brown the chicken in several batches if necessary.) Carefully regulate the heat to avoid scorching the skin. Then turn the pieces, season again with salt and pepper, and brown on that side, 5 minutes.

Remove the chicken pieces from the skillet, reduce the heat to medium, and add the sliced onions and garlic (adding more oil if needed to keep them from sticking). Cook, stirring frequently, until the onions are translucent, about 8 minutes.

Sprinkle the flour over the onions and cook, stirring, until the flour has absorbed much of the cooking juices and has a chance to cook, but not burn—at least 2 minutes.

Then return the chicken to the skillet, add the beer and the bouquet garni, stir, and bring to a boil. Reduce the heat and cook, partially covered, at a lively simmer until the chicken is cooked through, about 50 minutes. Remove the chicken from the sauce and return the sauce to a boil. Reduce it by half, until it has thickened to the consistency of thin gravy, 5 to 8 minutes.

Return the chicken to the sauce, and remove the skillet from the heat; set it aside. (The chicken can be prepared up to this point a day ahead. Refrigerate it, covered. The following day, skim off any fat that has congealed on the surface, if desired. Reheat, covered, over medium-low heat.)

ADDITIONS

1 tablespoon unsalted butter
Freshly ground salt and black pepper
1/2 pound bacon or pancetta
1 pound button mushrooms, brushed clean and cut into quarters
40 pearl onions, peeled
1 cup chicken stock
1/2 cup (loosely packed) curly parsley leaves, for garnish (optional)
Thyme sprigs, for garnish (optional)

While the chicken is cooking, prepare the additions: Melt the butter in a medium-sized heavy skillet over medium-high heat. Add the pearl onions, season lightly with salt and pepper, and sauté until golden, about 10 minutes.

Add the chicken stock, reduce the heat to medium, and cook at a lively simmer, shaking the pan occasionally so the onions cook evenly until they are tender through and the stock has nearly evaporated, about 20 minutes. Remove from the heat and keep warm.

Cut the bacon into small cubes. Brown it in a medium-sized heavy saucepan over medium-high heat. Remove the bacon with a slotted spoon or spatula and set it aside on a plate.

Drain off all but 1 tablespoon of the fat. Add the mushrooms to the pan and cook, stirring constantly, until they begin to give up their liquid, are slightly golden, and are nearly tender through, about 5 minutes. Season generously with pepper, and remove from the heat.

Add the mushrooms, bacon, and pearl onions, along with any juices, to the chicken; gently mix them in. Either transfer to a large warmed serving platter (one with edges, so the juice won't run off) or serve directly from the cooking pot.

Garnish with the parsley and thyme, if desired, and serve immediately.

—Adapted from Susan Herrmann Loomis's
French Farmhouse Cookbook, pages 127–28

Potjevleesch
(Veronique's Mother's Mixed Meat Terrine)
from the Nord/Pas-de-Calais Region

From an excerpt from my series *Savoring the Olde Ways* comes the story of Veronique and her mother, who live near Dunkerque (Dunkirk). Their love of Flemish cuisine gave rise to the addition of *Potjevleesch* to the novel and this companion cookbook.

At the Farmhouse of a Friend Near Dunkirk, 2002

Kate looked around the farmhouse kitchen. The far wall was filled with an enormous brick, walk-in fireplace. The crackling fire in the hearth lent warmth and charm to the low-ceilinged but otherwise darkened room. An ornate wrought-iron stove shored up another wall, while overhead herbs hung in strings from blackened beams along with sundry copper pots and pans. Hanging from a peg was a handwoven basket, which Veronique took down and began to layer with the warmed bread. Sophie finished setting the table and peered into the basket.

"Did I tell you that my father taught me to weave baskets like this, Kate?" Sophie asked.

As Kate was nodding in acknowledgment, Veronique said, "Is that right? My grandfather taught me to weave this one."

"They look like a similar weave. Oh, it does bring back such wonderful memories," Sophie said. "I'll have to tell you about it. Ah, but another time. Looks like we are ready to have our *quatre heure*."

"*Quatre heure?*" Kate asked. She looked at her watch and it was, indeed, four o'clock.

"Yes, we French," Sophie chirped, "are noted for eating any hour of the day, but a snack called the *goûter* is most welcome at four o'clock. This was the time when most schoolchildren had come home from an exhausting day at school. Being met with a savory and sweet *goûter* at that time of day was most welcome."

"We will have slices of chilled terrine that my mother has made," Veronique said as her mother placed gherkins and pearl onions onto a plate and set them on the table. "I am about to introduce you to my mother's most traditional dish. It is her famous *Potjevleesch*. Right, *Maman*? It is always served with a good, strong fermented beer. You do like beer, don't you Kate? Sophie?"

"Absolutely," Kate and Sophie said together.

"As much as I enjoy wine—and I do," Sophie said, "I love beer best—especially the wonderful beers you have here in the Nord/Pas-de-Calais." She repeated what she had said in French so that Madame Lund, who spoke only a few words of English, was included.

Madame Lund nodded vigorously and lifted her glass of beer in a connecting cheer. "*Tchin-tchin*," they all toasted.

"Now to begin, Kate, this Flemish specialty is called *Potche-Vletche* or *Potjevleesch* in Flemish," Veronique said, "which means 'meat pot.'" Kate had obviously told her she wanted recipes along with traditions, so Veronique was off like a mad hatter.

She picked up a slice of bread, smoothed on some of the terrine, took a bite, then bit into the pickle, then took a sip of her beer. She continued in this order until her plate was clean and the recipe had been divulged.

—*Savoring the Olde Ways*

4 chicken legs, deboned
1/2 pound veal shin
5 cloves garlic, chopped
3 sprigs thyme
1 tablespoon juniper berries
4 cups white wine or good Flemish beer
2 cups sliced onions
1/2 pound rabbit meat
1/2 pound boned pork loin
1 stalk celery, chopped
3 bay leaves
Freshly ground salt and pepper to taste
3 sheets of gelatin
8 slices bacon, cut into squares

Chop the four meats into large chunks, and then place them evenly into a large shallow glass dish. To prepare the marinade, place the chopped garlic and celery into a medium-sized mixing bowl. Add the thyme, bay leaf and juniper berries, salt and pepper, then pour in the beer or wine. Pour over the meat, cover, and leave in a cool place for 24 hours.

Preheat the oven to 300°F. Soften the 3 sheets of gelatin in cold water. Remove the meat from the marinade and layer the meat, with a sheet of gelatin between each layer into a terrine. Spread the onion rings and bacon squares over the top. Pour the marinade back over the meat and seal. Bake the terrine for 3 hours. Remove the terrine from the oven and allow to cool down slowly at room temperature before placing the terrine into the refrigerator for 12 hours to set. Cut into slices and serve cold as a main dish, with pickled gherkins, pearl onions, and toasted brown rye bread, or with French fries, a green salad and always a strong fermented beer.

*Veronique checked in on her mother's recipe and sent this by email: "One thing I remember when my mother prepared this dish is the meats (usually four different meats) had to be cooked all together *with* the bones; stewed till the bones could be removed easily from the meat. It was the bones that produced the natural gelatin to the dish, which held it together as well as flavored it. Now, we use gelatin sheets. It's much easier, but not always as tasty!"

Agneau Pré-Salé
(Pre-Salted Lamb)
from the Normandy Region

Across from Mont Saint-Michel, Normandy, 2001

As they drove along the banks of the *Baie du Mont Saint-Michel,* evening mist began to rise from the deep grasses, and the setting sun sent radiant shafts of golden light across the windows of a grey stone manor, which loomed before them. Following along a lime-tree-lined entryway, they pulled up to a four-story manor house covered in a thick beard of ivy. An ele-gant staircase, which swept down from the center of the house, held a bevy of young men who rushed down the steps to assist them. The women were hustled into the manor's main hallway where they were met by their hosts, the Barreaux, before being escorted four flights up to their room. Having driven across a large swath of France that day, they found this a welcome greeting.

Once they had settled in, Kate and Sophie made their way back down to the main dining room, where a large open-pit grill was set into the main house wall. The heady aroma of the house specialty, *Agneau Pré-Salé,* or roasted lamb, tantalized both Sophie and Kate.

"What is *Agneau Pré-Salé,* anyway?" asked Kate. They had ordered a bottle of local apple cider while awaiting their dining table.

"It's quite well known around here," Sophie replied. "The lovely lambs that graze by the bay consume salt-encrusted marsh grasses. The salt serves to season and flavor their meat, a very rare delicacy from this area."

—*A Cup of Redemption,* page 255

The following excerpt was taken once again from *Savoring the Olde Ways,* a soon-to-be-released travel cookbook. The characters remain the same.

"Yes, Monsieur Barreaux, Kate, here, is writing a book about families and their traditional values—especially when it comes to food," replied Sophie, steering them back to business. "Now, when did you become a chef? You are saying this hasn't always been your profession."

"No. But I always liked the cuisine. I am an *autodidacte,* or a self-made man. I never entered culinary school, but I do prepare the cuisine with my heart and feelings, more than by professional training. I have always prepared the food I like."

"In your cuisine, are you using family recipes?" Kate asked.

"I use some recipes of local tradition. Here, you must have noticed we have the lamb raised on salted pastures covered by the salt water of the sea on high tides."

"Yes, we ate your lamb for dinner last night, and it was absolutely succulent," Kate said.

"Ah, I'm so glad. You see, the salt produces a special variety of grasses, and the lambs raised on these pastures along the *Baie of Mont Saint-Michel* have a very special flavor and tenderness. Thus, the succulence that you mentioned. The lambs that graze around the clock during the summer and into the winter months are highly valued and are protected by an *Appellation d'Origine.* Each lamb is documented . . . has a tag and is sold with a certificate of authenticity. It is a very specific type of farming. The sheep farm where we purchase lamb produces only the special lamb called *Grevin.* It comes from the word *grève,* given to the strip of land going from low tide to high tide. And, as you know, we are known for having very high tides, up to forty-five feet, with the waters sweeping inland as far as nine miles. So it is up to the farmers to make certain that the lambs are moved twice a day to avoid peril."

"We noticed there are many tags hung by the fireplace. Are these tags from the lambs you prepared here?" Sophie asked him.

"Yes, this is the certification and guarantee of the product," Monsieur Barreaux responded proudly.

"And the recipe for your most marvelous *Agneau Pré-Salé*?" asked Sophie coyly.

"Ah, now, that must remain my secret," Monsieur Barreaux said with a wink and a smile.

—*Savoring the Olde Ways*

I won't be providing a recipe for *Agneau Pré-Salé*, except to advise that you find yourself a roast from a lamb originally raised as a *Grevin.* After it has been sufficiently basted with olive oil and sprigs of rosemary, roast it carefully in the oven. Of course, Monsieur Barreaux uses a spit and roasts the lamb directly over a live fire. Succulent, and truly délectable!

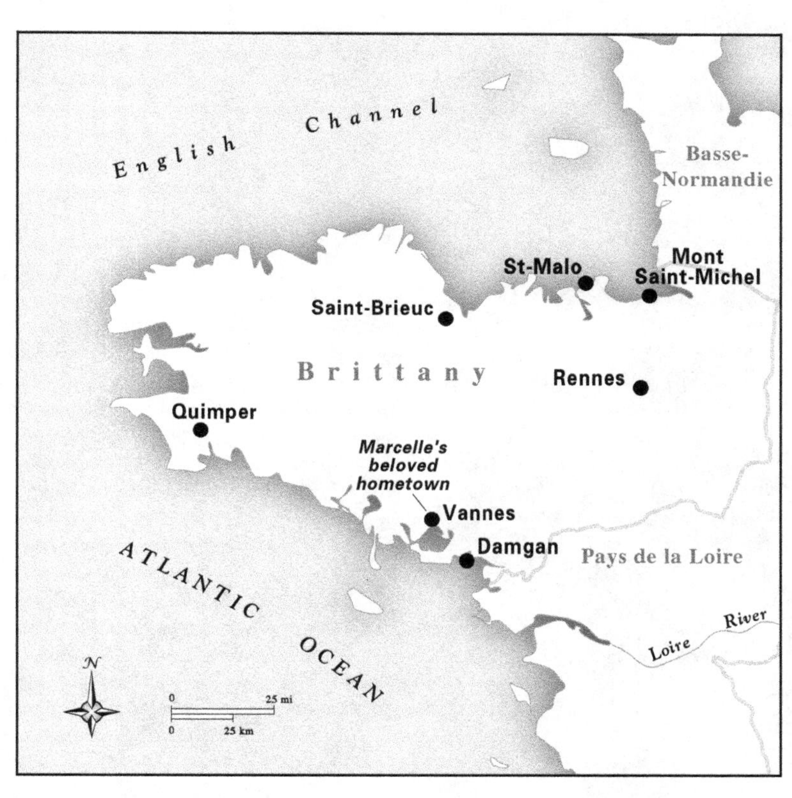
English Channel
Basse-Normandie
Mont Saint-Michel
St-Malo
Saint-Brieuc
Brittany
Rennes
Quimper
Marcelle's beloved hometown
Vannes
Damgan
Pays de la Loire
ATLANTIC OCEAN
Loire River
N
0 25 mi
0 25 km

CHAPTER SIXTEEN

Crêpes de Froment
AND
Moules avec Cidre et à la Crème

Crêpes de Froment
(Sweet and Savory Crêpes)
from the Brittany Region

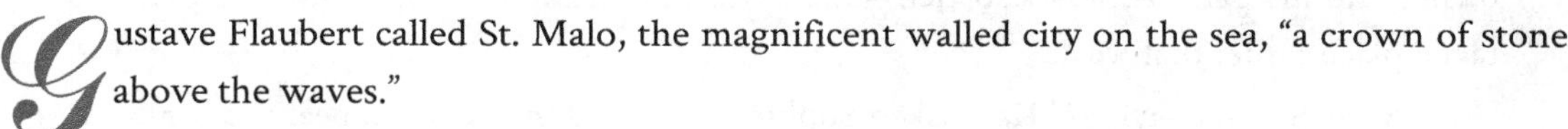

Gustave Flaubert called St. Malo, the magnificent walled city on the sea, "a crown of stone above the waves."

St. Malo, Brittany, 2001

As the two women ventured farther into Brittany, rain fell gently upon them, off and on, light and misty at times, changing slightly with the wind. The November air felt cool but not cold, so as they traveled around the fringes of Brittany's coastline, they popped in and out of the car enjoying the seascapes. It was early afternoon when they veered off the main road to stop in the walled city of St. Malo. The tide was extremely low. Old tugs and sailboats listed heavily to one side with their keels resting lazily in the mud. The two climbed from the car to follow a path where locals walked along the seawall with their dogs, stopped to chat with old friends, or disappeared through the city gates. Before the majestic Solidor Tower within the city wall, others sat quietly on park benches to smoke or ponder the day. Seagulls and pelicans skulked about the edges of the water in search of lunch, and the smell of salt, sea, and seaweed wafted up to the two as they sought out a *crêperie.*

—*A Cup of Redemption,* pages 265–66

As a special treat to you, my reader, I am including a part of this chapter that was cut from the original novel. It relates more of the story of the women, politics, and crêpes enjoyed in St. Malo. (This tour actually took place in April 2002)

"Hear that?" Kate asked. "I believe that's my stomach growling." Sophie, the quintessential tour guide, rose to the challenge. Kate's appetite was one she herself did not have but could certainly accommodate. She quickly moved back into her mode of taking charge, and off they went. *Vite! Vite!* Off to a number of little cafés that paralleled the water.

Unfortunately for them, it was nearing 2:00 p.m. and the cafés were preparing to close for the afternoon. Not to be daunted, Sophie asked for suggestions, and they were directed up the street to a little *crêperie.* As the door swung open and they entered the tiny shop, they were hit with the sweet smell of sizzling crêpes. The banter inside, between the owner and his patrons, was also rich—rich with talk of the national primaries that had taken place earlier that week.

"What are they saying?" Kate asked Sophie as they slid into a booth near the bar.

"The owner of the *crêperie* is saying, after eighteen years of flipping crêpes, mind you, he has made the decision this very week to sell his business and is also thinking of leaving the country as well. It appears Brittany is not far enough away from the fray of presidential politics!" Sophie said with a toss of her head and a hearty laugh.

"Nothing good could possibly come from either presidential hopeful," the owner intoned. "But we will know shortly, as the runoff is due in another week." He prepared crêpes at a fast clip as he bemoaned the thought of having to sell. "But then, what is a Frenchman to do? Enough is enough!" he wailed.

"I've never had a crêpe made in Brittany, the crêpe capital of the world," Kate whispered. She ordered two—*they're small,* she thought—a savory one with a bit of ham and cheese, and a sweet crêpe made with a red berry *confit* with butter drizzled throughout and sprinkled with powdered sugar. Sophie opted for a savory crêpe, as well. But only one! The crêpes were served hot, steaming actually, and the brown lacy pancakes melted into their mouths.

"Did I even chew?" Kate asked out loud. "A quick cup of coffee is definitely needed now," she added.

But while Kate had been totally engaged in eating, Sophie, like the Frenchwoman she was, was more interested in debating the issues of the contentious upcoming runoffs. Her laughter rang through the small café, and others joined in with her. She turned to Kate and said, "Just like I told you! People everywhere are planning to go to the polls with clothespins on their noses—just to show their disdain!" She laughed aloud. They all laughed, and their voices remained raised. "These people still live in France," Sophie said by way of explanation.

As the two slipped out the door, Sophie said, "Those are Frenchmen for you; they never miss a chance to debate politics! I love that about my countrymen."

—*Savoring the Olde Ways*

I have already given you a couple of recipes for crêpes in Chapter One, but those were some of the original buckwheat crêpes that came into being early on in Brittany. Later a finer, more delicate crêpe was concocted, and it is more to the liking of those who harbor a sweet tooth.

This batter is generally sweetened with Vanilla Sugar, but savory crêpes can be made from it as well. Just eliminate the sugar.

1 1/2 cups all-purpose flour
3/4 teaspoon salt
2 1/2 cups milk, divided
1 tablespoon Vanilla Sugar (recipe below)
3 large eggs
1 tablespoon melted butter
Red berry *confit* or any other jam available

Sift the flour and salt together into a bowl and make a well in the center. Add 1 1/4 cups of the milk (water will also work here, if you have no milk) and all the Vanilla Sugar, gradually whisking the flour into it. Add in the eggs, one at a time, whisking just until they are blended. Then whisk in the remaining milk. Let the batter sit for 30 minutes.

Heat a crêpe pan over medium-high heat. Brush the pan with some of the melted butter. Pour batter into the center, enough to spread thinly across the pan. Quickly shake the pan so the batter coats the bottom. Let the crêpe cook until golden, about 1 1/2 minutes. Lift the edge slightly and, using a wooden or plastic spatula, flip the crêpe to the other side. Cook for an additional 30 seconds. Place the crêpe on a warm plate, cover with a cotton tea towel, and set in a very low oven. Continue adding more crêpes until you have made enough for the family. Serve by rolling the little pancakes with soft butter and berry *confit* spread inside or drizzled on top.

SUCRE VANILLE (VANILLA SUGAR)

4 cups sugar
1 fresh vanilla bean

Pour the sugar into an airtight container with a lid and push the vanilla bean down into it. Cover and let ripen for at least 1 week. Replenish the sugar as you use it. Replace the vanilla bean once every 2 months.

—Adapted from Susan Herrmann Loomis's
The French Farmhouse Cookbook, pages 362–63

Moules avec Cidre et à la Crème
(Mussels with Cider and Cream)
from the Brittany Region

> "The Bretons were used to this cold, and living by and with the sea. Of course, they knew no different. As Bretons say about all of Brittany," continued Sophie, "*Me zo gañet é kreiz er mor*, which means, 'I was born in the middle of the sea.' I think that is one of the things my mother loved best about her native land: It was surrounded on three sides by the sea. Even though Brittany feels so removed, so remote, I believe, that was part of the identity—her inner identity—a kinship with the light and the melancholy." Despite the cold, the two women stood, facing the wind, until the sun dipped below the horizon.
>
> —*A Cup of Redemption*, page 271

Again, I treat you with an extract from *Savoring the Olde Ways* and an introduction into the delectable seafood of Brittany.

By this time it was getting to be early evening, so they stopped in the village of L'Etapes sur Mare, found a room, and asked for a good restaurant. They were directed to a folksy little establishment stuffed full of locals.

"Must be good food," Kate said, licking her lips in anticipation. In fact, the steamed mussels they shared that night, steeped in a rich, wine-based broth and topped with thick salted cream, were absolutely the best they each had ever eaten.

Sophie said, "Ah! We must be in Brittany—it's the cream!"

"Yes, this is exquisite, but I thought you said that about Normandy."

"*C'est vrai, aussi!*" Sophie said with a grin and a shrug of her shoulders.

—*Savoring the Olde Ways*

SERVES 4

4 pounds mussels
2 shallots, finely chopped
1 sprig each parsley, bay leaf, and thyme
4 ounces cream
1 clove garlic, finely chopped
2 tablespoons butter
4 ounces dry white wine or cider
1/4 cup freshly chopped parsley

Wash the mussels under plenty of cold, running water. Discard any open ones that won't close when lightly squeezed. Remove the fibrous beards protruding from between the tightly closed shells and then scrub the shells with a stiff vegetable brush. Give the mussels another quick rinse to remove any little pieces of shell.

Soften the garlic and shallots in the butter with the herbs, in a large pan big enough to take all the mussels—it should only be half full. Add the mussels and wine or cider, turn up the heat, then cover and steam them open in their own juices for 3 to 4 minutes. Give the pan a good shake every now and then.

Remove the bouquet garni and discard any unopened mussels. Add the cream and chopped parsley and remove from the heat. Spoon into four large warmed bowls and serve with lots of crusty bread.

—Adapted from several recipes in *Larousse Gastronomique*

CHAPTER SEVENTEEN

Kouign Amann
Belon Oysters
AND
Sole Meunière

Vannes, Brittany, 2001

The three turned at the Place des Lices and walked through a neo-Moorish archway, beautifully decorated with brightly colored enameled bricks. They were entering an immense indoor marketplace, which Mimi said was a blessing on days of inclement weather. Throughout the massive room were aisles filled with vendors —the butcher, the baker, the vintner, and the dairy farmer.

"Typical Breton products are displayed here, such as goat cheeses, or, more unusually, *pie-noire* cheeses made from the milk of the Breton cow," Sophie said.

"Oh, Kate, look over there," Mimi said, pointing to a number of women seated quietly on a bench near the door. "They are known as the *p'tites dames au beurre,* or the 'eggs and butter ladies.' They come each market day from surrounding villages with their wicker baskets filled with freshly churned butter and large farm eggs. Nothing better." She smacked her lips.

On tables and in cases, *Galette-saucisses* competed alongside Breton onion tarts, *Far Breton aux Pruneaux,* and *Kouign Amann.* Groups of jabbering women waited in long lines for their share of the tall stacks of freshly made *blé noire,* or buckwheat crêpes.

"It looks as if homemade crêpes are becoming a thing of the past," Kate observed. "Like convenience has once again taken a bite out of tradition!"

"Ah, but are we not so different from you, dear Kate?" Sophie asked with a smile and a shrug.

Kate nodded and grinned. "*C'est vrai! C'est vrai!*"

Before they knew it, Sophie and Kate entered into the fray, following quickly behind Mimi as she gathered up fresh bread, sweet buns, and local cheeses. They sampled wines and hard cider and were charmed by salesclerks wearing traditional Breton costumes. Sophie and Mimi took turns purchasing specialty charcuterie, including *Morlaix* ham and *Andouilles de Bretagne*, before darting out the door for the fresh vegetable and flower markets. Time was of the essence; the winter vegetables were being plucked up quickly.

With too much already in hand, the women finally reached the fish market, a freshly restored nineteenth-century hall. They threaded their way through the aisles, where table after table, continuing the full length of the hall, was covered with fresh ice and topped with mixed and a sundry fresh fish just pulled from the waters off Quiberon. On other tables were mountains of bulots, Belon oysters, clams, cockles, scallops, winkles, spiny lobsters, crabs, shrimp, and langoustine. Many of these creatures Kate had never seen before, and when Sophie and Mimi attempted an English derivative, they both came up short and burst into laughter. They picked up a dozen Belon oysters and three fillets of sole, all for the day's lunch, before trotting out the door.

—*A Cup of Redemption*, pages 281–82

Kouign Amann
(Breton Butter Cake)
from the Brittany Region

1 1/2 cups (less 1 tablespoon) unsifted flour
1 tablespoon cornstarch
1/2 teaspoon orange flower water
Pinch of salt
1/2 envelope dried yeast
1/2 cup lukewarm water
10 tablespoons lightly salted butter (a specialty of Brittany)
1/2 cup granulated sugar
1 egg yolk, slightly beaten

Put the flour and cornstarch into a bowl; add the orange flower water, salt, yeast, and lukewarm water. Work into a soft dough and flatten into a round cake, 1/2 inch thick by 6 inches in diameter. Set on a lightly buttered plate. Cover with plastic wrap and let rise until double in bulk.

Knead the butter with your thumb or fingers to make sure that it is soft and pliable. Have the sugar ready. Flatten the cake of dough into a small 6-inch square. Put the butter into the center, shaped as a 4-inch square that's 1/2 inch thick. Enclose the butter inside the dough. Let stand for 5 minutes. Roll the dough into a 12-inch-long flat band, keeping it 4 inches wide. Sprinkle with a third of the sugar. Pass the rolling pin over the sugar to press it into the dough. Fold the bottom of the dough toward the center, then the top to cover the bottom. Turn the dough 90 degrees so that it will now look like a book ready to open. Cover with plastic wrap once again and store in the crisper of the refrigerator for at least 20 minutes.

Take the dough out of the refrigerator and give it a second turn. Before closing the dough, sprinkle with the second third of the sugar. Fold and give a third turn. Before the third folding, sprinkle the last third of the sugar onto the dough, less 1 teaspoon. Refrigerate another half hour. Give a last turn and with the rolling pin tease the dough into a round cake as close as possible in size to an 8-inch or 9-inch cake pan. Transfer the dough to the cake pan—which you've slathered with butter. Dock (slash) the top of the cake into a crisscross pattern, cutting at least 1/4 inch deep into the dough.

Keep the cake at room temperature and let the dough rise within 1/4 inch of the edge of the cake pan. Brush the top of the cake with the egg yolk, sprinkle with the last teaspoon of sugar, and bake in a preheated oven at 375°F for 25 minutes. The top of the cake should be nice and golden, and on its bottom, a lovely buttered caramel layer will build. Serve warm and with a nice hot cup of coffee—or a bowl of café.

—Adapted from a recipe from Loetitia in
When French Women Cook by Madeleine Kamman, page 305

Belon Oysters
from the Brittany Region

Of all the oysters found in French waters, the most sought after are the Belons because of their delicate and nutty flavor. It has been said that as far back as the fourth or fifth century. the Romans noted their discovery of these most delicate and flavorful of all oysters as having come from the Armorican Sea, the old name for the Breton waters.

Marcelle, the main character in *A Cup of Redemption*, was born, raised, and celebrated her life where she lived right off that very Armorican Sea. Her grandfather taught her about the marvelous seafood that came from the sea, and he also wove many a haunting tale about the Celtic myths that rose from that same sea. Always remember Dahut!

Mimi, Sophie, and Kate ate their delicate Belon oysters raw with a spritz of vinegar, a sprinkling of shallots, and a slice of fresh lemon. Nothing could be simpler; nothing could be tastier.

Mimi's Sole Meunière
from the Brittany Region

Prior to the days of nonstick pans, fish had to be floured before it was pan-fried in butter, which accounts for the name of this dish—*la meunière* is a miller's wife or the female owner of a flour mill. The name still applies to any fish cooked in butter.

SERVES 3

3 sole, about 6 ounces each
Salt and freshly ground pepper
1/2 cup (1 stick) salted butter, divided
1 tablespoon fresh lemon juice
2 tablespoons chopped flat-leaf parsley
1 lemon sliced

The fish is a very simple preparation. Have the fishmonger clean and skin the sole. Rinse them and pat them dry with a paper towel. Season with salt and pepper.

Using two nonstick 10-inch skillets melt half the butter and cook the three sole for 4 minutes on each side; two in one pan, one in the other. Transfer the sole to three heated plates. Discard the cooking butter in one of the skillets and add the remaining butter. Add the lemon juice and let the butter melt over a very low heat. Pour this sauce over the sole; sprinkle with parsley, place lemon slices along the side and serve immediately.

—Adapted from *France: The Beautiful Cookbook,* page 93

CHAPTER EIGHTEEN

La Cotriade d'Armor

Once again in this chapter from *A Cup of Redemption,* Sophie and Kate struggled with the haunting stories of Marcelle's past; the subject of food did not arise. But before they left Brittany, they were delighted by stories Mimi told.

One of the reasons for the special connection between Marcelle and Micheline (or Mimi) was that they both had loved their childhood summers basking in the sunshine while prancing along the waters of the Morbihan Bay (the name means "Little Sea") in Brittany. Even though they were a generation apart, their memories were very similar, and when they were together this brought them raucous laughter and a great joy.

Brittany, 2001

[Mimi begins:] "Some of my most treasured memories were when I went fishing with my father. We would fish for shrimps with an *aveneau,* which is a special net used to catch the shrimps. And my father would also fish with a harpoon. He would look around the rocks and eventually would find a conger eel. They were about two meters long and very difficult to catch but because he was raised here, he knew all of their best tricks. I thought he was wonderful and I was so proud of him." Her eyes were glistening with the retelling. She leaned over and refilled Kate and Sophie's wine glasses.

"And we children would be standing in the water busily gathering the mussels and oysters. The crabs were also easy to catch," she said. "We would lift up the seaweed and with a special hook, would wiggle it about and shuffle the whole thing. The crabs would venture out and we would catch them. I remember there were some places—special fishing holes—that were a little better than others. We also used some special barrel-shaped crab pots, where the crabs could go in but could not get back out again. Oh! It was great sport!" She clapped her hands together as her blond hair bounced with her movement. It was as if she were that gleeful child once again.

"And when we took the fish home, my grandmother would make soup or stew from the fish. She especially prepared the *matelote*, a fish soup made with conger eel. But this soup is loaded with bones—very, very fine bones. So I remember it was difficult to eat without straining it."

"Straining it?" Kate asked.

"*Oui*. Through our teeth." She gritted her teeth together to indicate the method used and inhaled with a schlishing sound. Schlish, schlish, schlish.

"But one of my favorite fish stews was *La Cotriade d'Armor*. Fish caught along the Amorican Coast. Mmmh! Mmmh!

—*Savoring the Olde Ways*

Like bouillabaisse in the south of France or cioppino here in our own country, *Cotriade* can be as diverse a stew as the fishing villages and ports the fishermen sail into along the coast of Brittany. This is a stew concocted of whatever seafood is available at the time.

La Cotriade d'Armor
(Mimi's Grandmother's Fish Stew)
from the Brittany Region

SERVES 6

1/3 cup *saindoux* or lard
1 cup sliced white onions
2 pounds potatoes, cut into chunks
Salt and pepper to taste
4 pounds mixed fish, gutted, scaled, heads removed

Melt the *saindoux* or lard in a large (6-quart) pot and cook the onions until golden, about 5 minutes. Stir with a wooden spoon. Stir in the potatoes and salt and pepper. Then add water to cover all and simmer for about 15 minutes.

Add the fish to the simmering liquid beginning with the firmest of fish and working down to the least firm. Let the liquid return to simmering after each addition. Season with salt and pepper and simmer for 15 more minutes.

Remove the fish and potatoes with a slotted spoon and place in warmed bowls. Add a ladleful of broth and serve with dark bread. A dash of vinegar in the soup will lift the flavors. Enjoy!

—Adapted from *Culinaria France,* page 102

CHAPTER NINETEEN

Friture de la Loire AND *Rillettes du Mans*

Anger, Loire Valley, 2001

It was only midmorning [when they arrived in the Loire Valley], so Sophie encouraged Kate to take a tour of the Château d'Angers. "The last tour of the morning will probably begin shortly," she said. "I have to make some phone calls to arrange for our next stay, so why don't you go ahead. I'll be back here to pick you up in a couple of hours and we'll have lunch."

Kate numbly proceeded across the moat and over the drawbridge to the entrance gates of the castle. She purchased her ticket and stood in the inner courtyard near the formal gardens awaiting the beginning of the tour. The sunlight fell on her shoulders and warmed her chilled body . . . The tour took her into the feudal fortress, which, she learned, was built in the 1230s, by Blanche of Castille, the mother of Louis IX. Built of limestone and schist, the forbidding-looking building with its seventeen towers had remained grim in color and design until succeeding monarchs, such as King René I, had added the charm to the castle with gardens, aviaries, and a menagerie. Even though the fortress had faced many enemies, the tour guide touted, the Allied bombers wrought significant damage to the building during World War II, as the Germans were using it as a munitions base. World War II once again!

Kate realized she was in no mood to confront the past. She dropped off the tour to think more about Gérard's story, particularly the parts of his history that replicated her own. Wandering back into the sunshine of the formal gardens and away from the frigid dungeons and austere rooms of the fortress, she found a stone bench where she could sit and think.

—*A Cup of Redemption,* pages 305–06

In an excerpt from *Savoring the Olde Ways,* luncheon always became an important part of the story. The following is one of these luncheons in the Loire Valley:

> No mention was made of their earlier conversation as Sophie pulled away from the curb and took a left onto Boulevard du Roi René. En route, they stopped for a short lunch—probably the shortest they encountered at one and a half hours—in a hotel/restaurant establishment called Aubérge de la Rose. The sign outside indicated *Cuisine Traditionnelle et Raffinée.*
>
> "Have you been here before, Sophie?" Kate asked her as she did her best to keep up.
>
> "No, but when I see a sign like that, I know we will be able to find good traditional food inside. That's what you want to sample, isn't it?"
>
> "*Mais oui,*" Kate said, "but what is *raffinée*?"
>
> "That is the key word, *ma cherie*; it means 'refined' or 'sophisticated.' Sound good to you?"
>
> "But of course," Kate said, as they were quickly led through the dining room. White tablecloths covered small intimate tables; glass chandeliers sparkled above; mustard-yellow provincial printed wallpaper covered the walls, and matching damask curtains separated the dining area from the hotel.
>
> "After we share a plate of *Friture de la Loire* (similar to French-fried smelt, but is local fish from the Loire River), we will then proceed to share in a plate of *Rillettes du Mans,* which is usually shredded potted rabbit or goose. In this case, it is rabbit, which is served along with garden greens," Sophie said as she ordered.
>
> "An appropriate place for a rabbit to nest," Kate quipped.

Friture de la Loire
(Fried Fish of the Loire River)
from the Loire Valley Region

"For friture," Sophie began to explain, "is any fresh water fish between two and four inches in length, but plump round fish are the best because they cook more evenly than a flatfish and they have more meat on their feathery little bones. Usually a mixture of fish is necessary. It seems on this day, a local fisherman has netted some bream, ablets, and gudgeons, although I'm certain he was hoping to find the smaller sandre, or pike-perch, which is the most highly prized of the Loire fish." She touched her fingers to her lips and kissed them lightly.

Kate looked at her with a wide-eyed expression.

"Yes, you're wondering how I know all this, but then, I am from near here. Right?" Before Kate could protest, Sophie hurried on. "And, for these tiny fish to be cleaned, the sous chef must run the edge of a thin knife down the sides of each fish to slice off their stomachs. Because this is such a time-consuming venture very few restaurants prepare friture anymore. So, we are in for a special treat!" Just then a luscious platter covered in the tiniest of all little fish, lightly batter-fried, and drizzled with fresh lemon, arrived on their table.

—*Savoring the Olde Ways*

SERVES 4

2 pounds *whitebait, sperling,
or small smelts, cleaned,
(removing the heads, if desired) and dried*
1 lemon (or use Lemon Mayonnaise, on next page)

3/4 cup flour
1 tablespoon chopped flat-leaf parsley
6 cups vegetable oil
Kosher salt to taste

*Whitebait is a mixture of small fish. It is frequently available in fish stores, but it is a good idea to order it in advance.

In a large saucepan, set the oil over medium-high heat. Heat to 375°F (if you're using a candy thermometer), or test the temperature by adding a small bread cube to the oil: It should brown in 30 seconds.

In a plastic bag, combine the flour and a handful of cleaned fish. Twist the bag closed and shake to coat the fish. Remove the fish from the bag; set them in a colander and shake to get rid of any excess flour. Add the fish to the hot oil and fry until firm, about 1 minute. Remove with a slotted spoon to a warmed plate lined with paper towels. Repeat.

Fry the fish a second time, in batches, until crisp and brown, about 1 or 2 more minutes. Remove with a slotted spoon to a plate lined with paper towels. When all the fish is fried, place in a serving bowl. Season with salt, tossing the fish to season evenly. Sprinkle with the parsley. Serve hot, like French fries, but with lemon wedges or Lemon Mayonnaise.

LEMON MAYONNAISE (MAKES 1 CUP)

1 egg yolk	1 teaspoon Dijon mustard
Kosher salt, to taste	1 cup olive oil
1 tablespoon lemon juice, divided	

In a medium bowl, whisk together the egg yolk, 2 teaspoons of the lemon juice, the mustard, and a little salt. Whisk in the olive oil, a few drops at a time at first, then pour it in a steady thin stream while continuing to whisk. Stir in the rest of the lemon juice, and adjust the salt to taste.

Rillettes du Mans
(Pieces of Fried Seasoned Meat)
from the Loire Valley Region

> For those who have tasted them [rillettes], swoon at the mention. Like pâté but lighter and more flavorful, there is something about their heavenly texture and gently spiced flavor that wins the heart and palate.
>
> —Susan Herrmann Loomis,
> *The French Farmhouse Cookbook*, page 21

Cut up 5 pounds of fresh rabbit and pork into large dice. Heat 1 ounce of lard in a pan, add the diced meat, and cook lightly. Add 1/2 cup water. Cook gently until tender, stirring frequently to make sure that the meat does not stick to the bottom of the pan. When the meat pieces are nicely browned, drain them.

Put the rillettes into small stone jars and allow them to cool. When they are cold, pour a thin layer of liquid lard over them. Cover with white butcher's paper.

To serve: Spoon the array of meat onto a platter layered with plenty of garden greens. Serve with baguette slices. These are highly esteemed for their flavor.

—Adapted from *Larousse Gastronomique*, page 811

CHAPTER TWENTY

Auvergne Guenilles

AND

La Truffade Auvergnage

Auvergne Guenilles
(Jeannine's Cinnamon Pastries)
from the Auvergne Region

Thierry and Jeannine's Farmhouse, Auvergne, 2001

"Oh, Jeannine, it smells soooooo good in here!" Sophie said, taking her scarf from about her neck and unbuttoning her jacket.

Again a half smile crept across Jeannine's face. She went directly to the coffeepot and began filling it with well water and measuring out the coffee, before turning to chat with Sophie. They conversed easily in French, catching up on each other's activities and family tales. Kate, used to this awkward moment of first arrival, wandered around the room trying to imagine what life was like in this kitchen. She remembered Sophie telling her about this house and farm being passed down through generations in Jeannine's family. As she tried to judge the age of the house, her eyes scanned the stucco-coated walls and then up and over the cracks etched across the ceiling. The floorboards were well worn and uneven, but the room was spotless. A table covering that extended the full length of the table appeared to once have been dotted in light blue and yellow flowers, but was now almost completely white from wear and hard scrubbing. A small bouquet of sunflowers sat prominently in a pale green canning jar in the center. Sophie pulled out a chair and invited Kate to sit down. Once the coffee finished perking, Jeannine set cinnamon pastries [*Guenilles*] and steaming mugs of coffee before them and joined them at the table.

—*A Cup of Redemption,* page 319

2 1/4 cups all-purpose flour
1/4 cup granulated sugar
Pinch of salt
7 tablespoons soft butter
4 eggs
2 quarts peanut oil
1/4 cup castor sugar
1 teaspoon ground cinnamon

Sift the flour into a bowl. Add the sugar and a pinch of salt, followed by the softened butter, cut into cubes, and then the eggs. Mix to a smooth dough. Roll the dough out to a 1/4-inch thickness and cut into strips.

Fry the strips in hot peanut oil; drain on paper towels and sprinkle with cinnamon-sugar.

> "Guenilles" in French is a term that means rags, because of the shape of these doughnuts from the Auvergne are reminiscent of strips of cloth.

La Truffade Auvergnate
(Jeannine's Country-Fried Potatoes, Bacon, and Cheese)
from the Auvergne Region

The following morning, after a hearty breakfast worthy of farmhands—freshly baked bread, fried eggs, bacon, and *saucissons*—Thierry led Sophie and Kate out the back door and into his garden. With great pride he showed them a garden that was bounded on the edges with sunflowers and enclosed with heavy mesh fencing. He pointed out where he would plant his fresh sweet peas and asparagus in the spring and showed Kate where he planned to place his lettuce, radishes, squash, potatoes, and corn. Proudly, he showed them where his planned tomato plants would go, once the weather warmed next year. In

> addition to the vegetables and flowers he loved to plant, he had made a little bower with his flowering bushes. Flaming orange and burgundy-red leaves now ran amok throughout the backyard. "Future raspberries and blackberries will grow here, along with some table grapes," Thierry promised.
>
> —*A Cup of Redemption,* page 327

The Auvergne is noted for its array of splendid sausages and ham products. Most farmers in the past made their own sausages and in this case, so did Jeannine. But these high-quality products can now be purchased and eaten at any meal. One other famous specialty from Auvergne is the *Truffade Auvergnate.* It is a marvelous addition to breakfast, or becomes an entire breakfast or lunch. Preparing the dish with the best of the Auvergne's local products, including its famous cheeses, makes all the difference.

SERVES 6 (CAN BE BREAKFAST OR LUNCH FARE)

1/2 pound smoked lardons or bacon, cut into chunks (or substitute sliced *saucissons* or sausage)
1/4 cup (1/2 stick) butter, plus more as needed
1 white onion, thinly sliced
3 pounds russet potatoes, thinly sliced
1 pound cheese, preferably *Tome fraîche* from Auvergne

In a large nonstick skillet, cook the lardons or bacon (or sausage slices) in the butter until browned. Add the onion and sauté. Once the lardons and onion are cooked, remove them from the skillet with a slotted spoon and set aside.

Put the potatoes into the same skillet with a little more butter. Brown them slightly on all sides. Cover the pan and let them cook through on lowered heat for about twenty minutes.

Grate the cheese or cut it into chunks. Add it to the pan, along with the reserved lardons (bacon) and onion, and stir. Cover the pan once again and heat until the cheese melts evenly over the potatoes and lardons. Allow the potatoes and cheese to brown slightly. (A slightly brown crunchy cheese frill is a lovely bonus.) Turn out onto a heated platter and serve for breakfast or with a salad for lunch.

Note: Kate has been preparing this recipe for years, but was enlightened by Jeannine through her addition of the marvelous Auvergne semi-soft cheeses, *Tome fraîche.*

CHAPTER TWENTY-ONE

Chapon Sauté à la Crème

AND

Tarte aux Pommes

In no time at all, they all were called to the table for *déjeuner* [lunch]. Jeannine had prepared a roasted chicken [*Chapon Sauté à la Crème*], fresh from their own farm, along with new potatoes and home-canned green beans from their larder. Wine flowed freely as everyone caught up on old and new news, and in no time at all, they were enticed by one of Jeannine's apple tarts. A new pot of coffee had been prepared, so after the tart, and everyone had time to stretch, they each headed to the coffeepot to pour refills.

"Do you want to join us," Christian asked Kate. "The family conclave is about to begin."

"Thank you, but I'm going to take my cup and sit out in the sunshine and read. If you need me for anything, just give a holler. And, Sophie, I'll be in the garden," she called over her shoulder.

—*A Cup of Redemption,* page 338

Chapon Sauté à la Crème
(Jeannine's Sautéed Capon with Cream Gravy)
from the Auvergne Region

A capon (*chapon*) is a chicken that has reached a weight of no more than 5 pounds. In this case, that is what Jeannine chose to select from her chicken coop and prepare, lovingly, for her family. This is a much richer, yet similar version to the Sunday chicken dinners all of our mothers fried for us. And nothing can beat a good chicken gravy.

1/2 cup (1 stick) butter

1 five-pound capon, the fresher the better (in this case, it was straight-from-the-farmyard-fresh), cut into 6 pieces: 2 from the breast, and 4 from the thigh and legs

Salt and pepper to taste

2 tablespoons white flour

1/2 cup dry white wine

1 cup chicken broth

1 cup heavy cream

4 egg yolks

1 tablespoon lemon juice

Bouquet garni: parsley, bay leaf, thyme, celery, all tied together

Melt the butter in a large skillet. When it is foaming, sauté the capon pieces, turning often so they will not brown, but will turn golden. Sprinkle with salt and pepper and cook over medium heat for 25 minutes. Sprinkle with the flour and cook, covered, 10 minutes. Stir in the wine and broth, add the bouquet garni, cover, and cook slowly for 25 more minutes, until tender. Place the capon in a serving dish.

In a separate bowl, blend the cream and egg yolks well. Stir this mixture slowly into the cooking pan, off the heat to avoid curdling. Stir in the lemon juice, then strain the sauce through a fine sieve. Bring this sauce almost to a boil. Remove from the heat and stir well; the sauce should be just thick enough to coat the capon. Spoon it over the pieces of bird and serve along with the new potatoes.

—Adapted from *Antoine Gilly's Feast of France,* page 169

Tarte aux Pommes
(Jeannine's Apple Tart with Apricot Preserves)
from the Auvergne Region

PÂTÉ BRISÉE (TART SHELL)

1 1/2 cups unbleached all-purpose flour

1/4 teaspoon sea salt

7 tablespoons unsalted butter, chilled and cut into 7 pieces

6 tablespoons ice water, divided

Place the flour and salt in a food processor and process once to mix. Add the butter and process until the mixture resembles coarse meal, pulsing 5 to 8 times. Add 5 tablespoons of the ice water and pulse just until the pastry begins to hold together, no more than 9 to 10 times. Add the remaining 1 tablespoon of water if the pastry seems dry.

Transfer the pastry from the food processor to your work surface and form it into a flat round. Let it rest, covered with a tea towel, for at least 30 minutes and as long as 1 hour. The pastry is now ready to be used.

For this recipe, you will need to prebake the tart shell. Roll out the pastry on a lightly floured work surface to form an 11 1/2-inch round, to fit a 10 1/2-inch tart pan with a removable bottom. Transfer the pastry to the pan, fitting it against the bottom and sides. Refrigerate the tart shell for an hour.

Preheat the oven to 425°F. Remove the tart shell from the refrigerator. Prick the bottom all over with the tines of a fork, and line it with aluminum foil. Fill the foil with pie weights or dried beans, and bake the tart shell in the center of the oven until the edges begin to turn golden, 10 to 15 minutes. Remove the tart shell from the oven and let it cool slightly before proceeding with the rest of the recipe.

FILLING

1 large egg
1/4 cup sugar
1/3 cup *crème fraîche* or heavy whipping cream
1 teaspoon vanilla extract
1/3 cup homemade jam apricot jam
2 medium-sweet apples, such as Jonagold, Cortland, or Gravenstein, cored, peeled, and cut into 1/2-inch-thick slices

Preheat the oven to 375°F. In a small bowl, whisk together the egg, sugar, *crème fraîche*, and vanilla.

If there are large pieces of apricot in the jam, chop them into smaller pieces. Spread them over the bottom of the prebaked tart shell. Then arrange the apples in concentric circles on top, overlapping the apples as you go.

Pour the cream mixture over the apples. It is a small amount; not to worry about spillage. Place the tart on a baking sheet and bake in the center of the oven until the apples are golden and the cream is firm, 35 to 40 minutes.

Remove the tart from the oven, and remove the sides of the pan. Place the tart on a wire rack and let it cool to room temperature before serving.

—Adapted from Susan Herrmann Loomis,
The French Farmhouse Cookbook, pages 435–36

CHAPTER TWENTY-TWO

Les Escargot du Pays Haut

(Julien's Snails from the High Country)
Lorraine Region

Lorraine, 2001

The ramshackle old building stood at the corner of Pont and LeDeau, in the old river section of the small town. Teetering on its moorings, one half of the building listed toward the river while the other half struggled to stay dry. It must have been a century-old wrestling match, but the tavern remained intact—at least for the time being. Julien hesitated outside the bar, then, after sizing up the thickness of the door, swung it open, hard. He lost hold of the handle, and as an entry to the bar and as a surprise to the occupants, the door slammed against the wall with a loud crash. Sheepishly, Julien smiled and strode toward the bar. The bartender resembled a skeletal version of his own father. Possibly a long-lost uncle, Julien surmised. He nodded in apology and moved in closer to the bar. The small den of a room held tight to the odors of the past century. One hundred years of stench from spilled beer; one hundred years of filth from clouds of cigarette smoke; and one hundred years from the reek of bad greasy food—fortunately prepared out of sight of the bar.

Julien hesitated in announcing his name or his mission and ordered a beer instead. It was midmorning and certainly not his practice to drink beer at that hour, but he was on a mission. He settled on a bar stool in the center of the five rickety stools available. A handful of patrons eyed him suspiciously before dropping their eyes to their cigarettes and beer. A light-blue haze billowed above them. They resumed whatever conversation he had stopped on his raucous entry.

—*A Cup of Redemption,* page 350

Okay, so I admit this previous scene doesn't conjure up a place for a délectable delight of sorts. In fact, it probably moves you to a room other than the kitchen. Yet just across the street and down the road from this bar was a spot where one of France's most exemplary culinary specialties was celebrated. This specialty came in the form of the lowly snail: the escargot. *La Fête aux Escargots*! And in fact, it was this same gentleman, Julien, who himself participated in this culinary feast as a boy.

La Fête aux Escargots was a great celebration most often held on the first of May in a community close to Ste. Barbe. Now only the old-timers remember it well, as the French government stopped the practice of collecting snails until into the summer months—much to many Frenchmen and women's chagrin.

First came the job for the men and boys:

Every year the men and boys of each family, including Julien and his father, would go out into the woods and countryside and collect thousands of snails. If you bent down and peeked through the thicket, you could see a large burlap bag being dragged behind every escargot catcher, through the woods, up the riverbanks, alongside the bubbling brooks, or wrapping itself around a tree as the escargots could be found there, too, clutching desperately onto the bark. When the bags were filled, the men and boys would head back home. Once back home, the escargots were left for about three days to fast, in order to expel any bad juices.

Next came the jobs for the mothers and daughters:

The women would scrub each snail shell with a stiff brush to extract the dirt. Then the snails and shells were boiled in a stock of water, herbs, and salt for just a few minutes. The snails were gingerly removed from their shells, and their bodies carefully cleaned. The toughest part of the snail was clipped off, and then they were returned to a new bath of white wine, onions, carrots, thyme, bay leaves, salt, and pepper. While they cooked (maybe an hour?), the shells were cleaned by thoroughly brushing the insides and boiling them. This was a long arduous process, taking hours and hours, because there were hundreds—maybe thousands—to prepare.

Now it was time for the garlic butter. This was usually made by Julien and Sophie's father, who would mix softened butter with parsley, minced garlic, salt, and pepper. (When Sophie made this—a process she learned from her father—she used a couple of sticks of butter and half a head of garlic, or sometimes more.)

When the butter mixture was completely blended, the shells and escargots were ready to assemble. First the cook would take one shell, place a small amount of Riesling wine in the bottom, add the escargot, and then a small knob of the herb butter. This was placed in a large pan and adjusted so that when the snails were baking the butter did not run out. The snails were baked in the oven at 350°F for 15 minutes. Then it was time to eat them, with plenty of good bread and a bottle or two of wine. Sometimes one, two, three, or even four dozen escargot per person!

Annie and Yvon from Chapter Eleven brought out a newspaper article written about *La* Fête *aux Escargots* back in 2000. It is very similar to Julien's version. But because both Annie and Yvon were asked for their recipe, they are the main contributors to this article:

Les Escargots du Pays Haut
(The Snails of the High Lands)

Only just a few years ago, each first Sunday of May, in a small Lorrain village of the Pays Haut, life was centered on the yearly Fête des Escargots, the Escargot Festival. From miles away people came to taste the famous gourmet delicacy. About 18,000 to 25,000 of these gastropods were prepared for the greatest pleasure of the "connoisseurs." Anne-Marie and Yvon gave us this very appreciated recipe:

"In the old days these 'animals' were picked up in the fields. First their inner 'system' had to be cleaned out. We had them fast for about three to four days, in a big bucket. Then we dipped them in a big pot of cold water, brought it to a boil to rid the escargots of most of the slime. The next step was to pull the snail out of its shell, cut off the inedible intestinal part, to keep only the foot or sole of the escargot. The remaining part of the escargot was rubbed with coarse salt. It was a long operation, repeated until all slime had been eliminated, and it would leave your hands red and sore for three to five days.

"Once cleaned, the snails were cooked for about one hour, in a stock prepared with water, thyme, bay leave, salt, pepper, onion, and—this was the special touch from Annie—a little bit of Riesling wine. Today, it is much easier; we buy the escargots in a can, ready to use!"

—Local Pays Haut newsletter

Escargot Butter

Makes enough for about 10 dozen escargots

4 sticks unsalted butter
1/2 cup parsley, finely chopped
8 garlic cloves, finely chopped
1/2 cup of shallots, finely chopped
3 teaspoons salt
3/4 teaspoon peppercorns, crushed
1 bottle of Riesling

Soften the butter; add the finely chopped parsley, chopped garlic and shallots. Mix thoroughly; add the salt and crushed peppercorns. Traditionally the snail's shells were used to serve the escargots. They had to be cleaned, which was an enormous task. It is now much easier to use dishes specially designed for the presentation of escargots. Place one escargot in one shell (or whole in a dish), splash a bit of Riesling in and generously cover it with the butter-garlic mix (approximately 1 tablespoon). Preheat the oven to 325° to 350°F and bake the escargots until the butter is bubbly. About 10 minutes. This "enchanting delicacy" should be served immediately, with another bottle of excellent Riesling wine.

Advice from Annie: "Do not eat escargots too often… You must watch your weight!"

CHAPTER TWENTY-THREE

Tourte de Viande Auvergnate

Tourte de Viande Auvergnate
(Marie Chirade's Pork and Veal Pie)
from the Auvergne Region

Auvergne, 2001

The next day, Marie Chirade had invited Sophie and Kate back to her home for *déjeuner* and after an hour of conversation, Marie led the two into her kitchen for a meal of *Tourte de Viande,* pork and veal pie made with puff pastry. The rich aromas that had whetted their appetites over the past hour were exchanged for savory flavors, which now filled their mouths with delight.

"Oh, Marie, this is divine!" Sophie blurted out. "I remember my mother preparing this many times when we were children, but I doubt that I've had it since. Did you teach her this recipe? This is so good! Don't you just love this, Kate?" Sophie asked jubilantly without waiting for a response.

"When we were growing up, sometimes we didn't have the specified meat for this dish, so *Maman* would use leftover *lard maigre*"—she turned to Kate—"which is lean grease. My father loved it, but I didn't. Too much fat, so this is superb!"

—*A Cup of Redemption,* page 357

Tourte de Viande Auvergnate is a traditional yet elaborate baked meat pie with a *pâté brissée* (pie dough) base and a puff pastry top. Ten minutes before the end of the baking period, a savory egg-and-cream custard is poured through a hole (chimney) in the piecrust and the dish returned to the oven to set.

4 ounces fresh pork, medium diced
4 ounces veal, medium diced
1 cup Riesling
Salt and pepper
*Quatre épices**
2 shallots, minced
2 cloves garlic, minced
1 onion, minced
2 bay leaves
2 sprigs thyme
4 cloves
Parsley, chopped
4 ounces *pâté brissée* (pie dough: see Chapter Twenty-One)
4 ounces puff pastry
1 egg plus 1 egg yolk
1/2 cup heavy cream
Nutmeg

Marinate the diced meat in the Riesling, salt, pepper, *quatre épices*, shallots, garlic, onion, and herbs for 48 hours.

After 48 hours, preheat the oven to 400ºF. Prepare the pie dough, then press it into a buttered and floured pie pan lined with parchment paper.

Place the meat on the pie dough, leaving a narrow border all around the edge. Roll out the puff pastry into a round to cover the pie. Cut a small round hole for the chimney opening in the middle of the dough, moisten the edges with a little water, and place it onto the pie, pressing the edges onto the crust. Brush the surface with beaten egg yolk. Make a small chimney in the middle hole by using a tube of cardboard covered with foil. Bake for 45 minutes.

While the pie bakes, beat the egg and yolk with the cream. Season with grated nutmeg, salt, and pepper.

Remove the pie from the oven and, with the help of a funnel, pour the cream mixture through the chimney. This operation is a bit delicate. You need to add a little at a time and then tilt the pan to disperse the liquid throughout the pie. Return the pie to the oven for 10 minutes before serving.

—Adapted from *Cookbook: Cuisine of France* (WikiBooks.org)

*Literally meaning "four spices," *quatre épices* is a spice mix used mainly in the French kitchen, but it's also found in some Middle Eastern kitchens. The spice mix contains ground pepper (white, black, or both), cloves, nutmeg, and ginger. Some variations use allspice instead of pepper or cinnamon in place of ginger.

The blend typically uses a larger proportion of pepper (usually white pepper) than the other spices, but some recipes suggest using roughly equal parts of each.

In French cooking, *quatre épices* is typically used in soups, ragouts, pot-cooked dishes, vegetable preparations, and charcuterie, such as pâté, sausage, and terrine, including this *Tourte de Viande.*

CHAPTER TWENTY-FOUR

Café Français

She reached down and scooped up the paper bag. Raising it before her, she pulled out a large, somewhat cracked, blue ceramic coffee cup. She stepped forward, placed the cup on top of her mother's headstone, and patted it with affection.

"There you go, *Maman,*" she said with reverence. "Our final tradition. May you continue to savor your coffee throughout eternity!" She smiled and stepped back.

—*A Cup of Redemption,* page 383

In a conversation between Sophie and Kate, Sophie enlightens Kate with a better understanding of the simple word: *café*: "The term *café* refers to both the coffee drink and the place where it is served—and French cafés serve some of the world's best coffee (or *café*)."

But, because each of us has our own coffee preferences, and a language barrier could possibly interfere with you ordering your favorite coffee, it might be important to understand what coffee drinks are on the French menu. If you can't have caffeine, this could be even more crucial.

The French Coffee Drinks

Café – is plain coffee with nothing added. It is strong, as it is brewed like espresso.

Café au lait – is a popular French coffee style that is coffee with steamed milk added, and it's almost always wonderful. Sometimes you may be served the coffee in a pot or in the cup, and then a pitcher of steamed milk is given to you on the side to pour in as you please.

Café crème – is, as it sounds, coffee served in a large cup/bowl with hot cream. (In many regions of France, morning coffee [café] is served in bowls.)

Café décafféiné – is decaffeinated coffee. You will still need to tell them you want milk or cream with your coffee.

Café Americain – is filtered coffee, similar to traditional American coffee; or, as in the coffee shop in the Louvre, it is often known as "weak coffee."

Other French Coffee Terms

Here are other terms that will come in useful when ordering coffee or visiting a French café:

Sucre – sugar. You can request this, although cafés typically bring a cup with two cubed sugars on the dish. Since French coffee is strong, you may want to request more: "*Plus de sucre, s'il vous plaît*"

Chocolat chaud – hot chocolate.

—Adapted from FranceTravelPlanner.com

BIBLIOGRAPHY

Antoine Gilly's Feast of France: A Cookbook of Masterpieces in French Cuisine by Antoine Gilly and Jack Denton Scott (Thomas Y. Crowell Company, 1971).

chocoparis.com/2011/10/gateau-au-chocolat-de-nancy.

Cookbook: Cuisine of France
(en.wikibooks.org/wiki/Cookbook :Cuisine_of_France).

Culinaria France by André Dominé (Könemann, 1999).

France: The Beautiful Cookbook: Authentic Recipes from the Regions of France by Gilles Pudlowski (HarperCollins San Francisco, 1989).

francetravelplanner.com.

The French Family Feast: Celebrating the Best of Traditional Dishes by Mireille Johnston (Simon and Schuster, 1988).

The French Farmhouse Cookbook by Susan Herrmann Loomis (Workman Publishing, 1996).

"L'Alsace Gourmande," a poem by Georges Spetz, 1913.

Larousse Gastronomique: The Encyclopedia of Food, Wine & Cookery by Prosper Montagné (Crown Publishers, 1961).

Les Meilleures Recettes des Régions de France by Paul Bocuse (Flammarion, 2002).

theworldwidegourmet.com/recipes/guenille-auvergne-doughnut.

When French Women Cook: A Gastronomic Memoir by Madeleine M. Kamman (Ten Speed Press, 1976).

INDEX OF RECIPES

Alsace Recipes

Auvergne Recipes

Brittany Recipes

Champagne Recipes

Loire Valley Recipes

Lorraine Recipes

Nord/Pas-de-Calais Recipes

Normandy Recipes

Paris/French Recipes

Acknowledgments

To my dear, sweet husband, Winston, who has been my most ardent supporter of this late-in-life adventure as a writer, and for his unfailing encouragement of me to continue to ride this wave—especially with recipes. Thank you, dear love of mine!

To the memory of Marcelle Zabé, who inspired not only *Recipes for Redemption: A Companion Cookbook to A Cup of Redemption,* but was the muse for my historical novel, *A Cup of Redemption.*

And to all of my French friends who enthusiastically offered their favorite recipes, including Josiane Selvage, Veronique Gindre, Jean-Claude and Martine Zabée, Jacky and Micheline Zabé, Micheline Thomas, Karine Foucher, Christine Lochert, Jeannine Pourrez, plus Anne-Marie and Yvon Peyrot. All came to my rescue to dig through their own or their mother's recipe boxes to find these beloved treasures. Because of their efforts I offer my deepest gratitude.

About the Author

photo credit: Bennington Photography

Carole Bumpus, a retired family therapist, is the author of the historical novel *A Cup of Redemption*, published October 2014 through She Writes Press. She is a state board and branch member of the California Writers Club's San Francisco/Peninsula Branch and has been published in three CWC short-story anthologies: *Fault Zone: Words from the Edge, Fault Zone: Stepping up to the Edge*, and *Fault Zone: Over the Edge*. She continues to write a travel blog taken from excerpts of her interviews with French and Italian families, Savoring the Olde Ways, and her articles on both food and US WWII veterans in France have been published in both the US and in France.

SELECTED TITLES FROM SHE WRITES PRESS

She Writes Press is an independent publishing company founded to serve women writers everywhere. Visit us at www.shewritespress.com.

A Cup of Redemption by Carole Bumpus. $16.95, 978-1-938314-90-2. Three women, each with their own secrets and shames, seek to make peace with their pasts and carve out new identities for themselves.

Tasting Home: Coming of Age in the Kitchen by Judith Newton. $16.95, 978-1-938314-03-2. An extraordinary journey through the cuisines, cultures, and politics of the 1940s through 2011, complete with recipes.

Hedgebrook Cookbook: Celebrating Radical Hospitality by Denise Barr & Julie Rosten. $24.95, 978-1-938314-22-3. Delectable recipes and inspiring writing, straight from Hedgebrook's farmhouse table to yours.

Seasons Among the Vines:Life Lessons from the California Wine Country and Paris by Paula Moulton. $16.95, 978-1-938314-16-2. New advice on wine making, tasting, and food pairing—along with a spirited account of the author's experiences in Le Cordon Bleu's pilot wine program—make this second edition even better than the first.

Away from the Kitchen: Untold Stories, Private Menus, Guarded Recipes, and Insider Tips by Dawn Blume Hawkes. $24.95, 978-1-938314-36-0. A food book for those who want it all: the menus, the recipes, *and* the behind-the-scenes scoop on some of America's favorite chefs.

www.ingramcontent.com/pod-product-compliance
Lightning Source LLC
Chambersburg PA
CBHW081743291224
19583CB00004B/64

9 781631 528248